Family
COOKBOOK

Ideals Publishing Corp.
Milwaukee, Wisconsin

CONTENTS

ISBN 0-89542-628-5

Copyright © MCMLXXII by Ideals Publishing Corporation
Milwaukee, Wisconsin
All Rights Reserved. Printed and Bound in U.S.A.
Published simultaneously in Canada

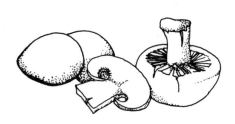

Crab Stuffed Mushrooms

3 dozen large whole fresh mushrooms
1-7½ ounce can crabmeat, drained and flaked
1 tablespoon snipped parsley
1 tablespoon pimiento, chopped
1 teaspoon chopped olives
¼ teaspoon dry mustard
½ cup mayonnaise

Wash and dry mushrooms. Remove stems. Mix all ingredients. Fill each cap. Bake 8 to 10 minutes at 375°

Millie Kusnier

Fried Cheese Puffs

Mix together 3 cups grated cheese, 2 tablespoons flour, ¾ teaspoon salt, and dash of pepper. Add 4 egg whites beaten stiffly. Form into balls, roll in cracker crumbs. Fry in deep fat.

These can be made ahead and stored in refrigerator, ready to be deep fat fried.

Mrs. Paul A. Beam

Ham-Cheese Ball

3 packages cream cheese (8 ounce packages)
1 cup diced ham bits
2 tablespoons horseradish
2 tablespoons mustard
2 cups finely chopped nuts

Combine first four ingredients and form in 3 or 4 inch balls. Roll in nuts. Delicious with crackers.

Mary Jane Ricks

Glazed Meatballs

1 pound ground beef	1 teaspoon salt
½ cup dry bread crumbs	⅛ teaspoon pepper
⅓ cup minced onion	½ teaspoon Worcestershire sauce
¼ cup milk	¼ cup shortening
1 egg	1 bottle (12 ounce) chili sauce
1 tablespoon snipped parsley	1 jar (10 ounce) grape jelly

Mix ground beef, crumbs, onion, milk, egg and next four seasonings. Gently shape into 1 inch balls. Melt shortening in large skillet; brown meatballs.

Remove meatballs from skillet; drain off fat. Heat chili sauce and jelly in skillet until jelly is melted; stirring constantly.

Add meatballs and stir until coated. Simmer 30 minutes. Serve hot in chafing dish. You may put toothpicks in a few of the meatballs and place a dish of toothpicks beside chafing dish for guests to use.

This recipe makes 5 dozen meatballs.

Nancy W. Burns

Shrimp Mold

Melt in top of double boiler, and cool:
- 1 can condensed tomato soup
- 1-8 ounce package cream cheese

Add:
- 2 envelopes gelatin, diluted in ½ cup cold water
- ½ cup minced onion
- ½ cup chopped celery } Chop fine
- ½ cup chopped green pepper
- 1 cup mayonnaise
- 3 cans (small) shrimp (tiny size)

Mix well and pour in greased mold. Chill at least 24 hours. Serve unmolded with flavored crackers or rye bread rounds (cocktail size).

Mrs. John F. Allen

Chicken Livers Paté

- ½ pound chicken livers
- 2 hard-cooked eggs
- ⅛ teaspoon pepper
- ½ teaspoon Worcestershire sauce
- 2 tablespoons cream
- 2 tablespoons butter
- 1 teaspoon salt
- ⅛ teaspoon celery salt

Cut livers in small pieces and cook in butter in skillet until lightly brown. Put livers and eggs through food chopper using fine blade. Add remaining ingredients and mix until smooth.

Dorothy Piepmeyer

Parsley Tomatoes

Cut tomatoes in generous slices. Chill and marinate in oil and vinegar dressing. Sprinkle with minced parsley.

Smoked Beef Dip

Soak 1 teaspoon minced onion in 1 tablespoon sherry until soft.

Add:
- 1 large package cream cheese
- 2 tablespoons mayonnaise
- ¼ cup stuffed olives, minced
- 1-3 ounce package smoked beef, minced

Delicious served with crackers or potato chips.

Mrs. Roger C. Wilder

Hot Shrimp Dip

- 1 can cream of shrimp soup
- 1 cup shredded sharp cheese
- ¾ cup shrimp, cut up (baby or broken shrimp)
- ¼ teaspoon tabasco sauce

In a saucepan, combine all ingredients and heat slowly, stirring until blended and mixture bubbles. Pour into fondue dish and serve as a hot dip with melba rounds. Makes 2 cups.

Ginger Williams

Chive Cheese and Almond Dip

- 6 ounce package chive cream cheese
- ¼ cup milk
- ¼ teaspoon salt
- 1 teaspoon prepared mustard
- ½ cup chopped toasted almonds

Soften cheese with milk. Mix in rest of ingredients.

Serve with raw green pepper, radishes, carrots, celery and cauliflower.

Millie Kusnier

5

 # JAMS AND JELLIES

Tomato Preserves

*Transparent flame, gold flecked,
Imprisoned in glass!*

In a steel or enamelware kettle put:
    4 cups of red-ripe tomatoes, peeled and finely cut

Heat slightly, pouring off a generous cupful of the juice that forms. (Save this juice to use as a vitamin-rich, low-calorie soup or spaghetti sauce base.)

To the tomatoes add:
    $1\frac{1}{2}$ teaspoons pickling spices, these tied in a square of cheesecloth or muslin.
    $\frac{1}{4}$ teaspoon powdered ginger
    2 cups sugar
    1 lemon, thinly sliced.

Simmer slowly, stirring often, until tomatoes become transparent . . . about 20 minutes. Set kettle off heat. Cover and let stand.

12 to 18 hours later:
    Reheat and simmer slowly for 30 minutes. Stir frequently, as it scorches easily.

After removing the sack of pickling spices, pour mixture into small jars, sealing each with paraffin. This recipe makes three cups of preserves and a lot of happiness for those to whom it is served with dark bread or graham rolls.

Mrs. A. R. Bergantine

Peach-Orange Marmalade

1 dozen large or 15 small peaches
1 orange (whole orange, including rind)
    Medium sized jar of maraschino cherries
    Sugar

Cut peeled peaches in small pieces and grind cherries and orange (also rind). Mix together and for every cup of fruit mixture add an equal amount of sugar. Cook one hour. Spoon into jars. Makes about 9 jars of marmalade.

"This is an old family recipe, usually made by my grandmother. The jars of marmalade disappear in a short period of time. This recipe is a blue ribbon winner at our county fair every year."

Patty Doarn

Rhubarb Jam

4 cups diced rhubarb
4 cups sugar

Stir above over low heat until dissolved. Bring to a rolling boil, then turn off heat.

Stir in 1 package cherry or strawberry Jello.

Let set 10 minutes. Seal in your jars.

Mary Biegel

Honey Jelly

$2\frac{1}{2}$ cups honey
$\frac{3}{4}$ cup lemon juice
$\frac{1}{2}$ cup liquid pectin

Combine lemon juice and honey. Bring to full rolling boil. Add pectin, stir and boil for two minutes longer. Pour into sterilized jars and seal with paraffin.

Mrs. J. H. Blackburn

Summer to Keep

Lee Avery

Put up the best of summer . . . As you keep its vivid fruit-like jewels in a jar . . . Conserve the gull-fleet moments that soar by . . . Enclose the pine that held an evening star . . . The clean delight that swept a beach at dawn . . . The sky that lifted with the flashing wings . . . Gather them to you while they still are fresh . . . Store up each beauty as it lifts and sings!

Frozen Strawberry Jam

2 cups strawberries, crushed
1 box pectin plus ¾ cup water
4 cups sugar

Prepare jars. Prepare fruit. Measure sugar, add to fruit and mix well. Combine ¾ cup water and pectin in saucepan. Bring to boil and boil for 1 minute, stirring constantly. Stir into fruit mixture. Continue stirring 3 minutes. A few sugar crystals will remain. Quickly ladle into jars. Cover at once with tight lids (no paraffin necessary). Set at room temperature about 24 hours. Then store in freezer. Ready to eat in 3 weeks.

Lanita Fleischmann

 SOUPS

Steak Soup

1½ cups steak, cut fine
1 cup carrots, cut fine
1 cup celery, cut fine
1 cup onions, cut fine
1 cup frozen mixed vegetables
2 tablespoons butter
1 can #303 tomatoes
1 cup flour
8 cups water
2 tablespoons beef base
1 teaspoon freshly ground coarse black pepper

Sauté steak in skillet until it is half done. Cook fresh vegetables in small amount of water until half done. Melt butter in large kettle, add flour and mix until smooth, add the 8 cups water and cook, stirring until done and smooth. Then add all ingredients together and simmer slowly for 1 hour. This is a good hearty soup.

Mrs. Floyd Olson

There is no spectacle on earth more appealing than that of a beautiful woman in the act of cooking dinner for someone she loves.

Thomas Wolfe

Tasty Garnishes On Soup

Grated cheese
Crumbled bacon bits
Toasted slivered almonds on creamed soups
Lemon slice on clear tomato
Minced parsley or chives on any cream or jellied soup
Cheese popcorn on tomato soup
Toasted garlic flavored croutons
Sprinkled paprika, nutmeg or cayenne pepper on cream soups

Chicken Corn Soup

Cut up and cook one whole chicken in enough water to cover it. After it is well-cooked, remove the chicken from the broth, remove the meat from the bones and cut it up fine and return it to the broth. Add 1 large, diced onion, 1 stalk of diced celery, 3 diced, hard-cooked eggs. Add as much whole-kernel corn as you want. (I use one large bag of frozen whole-kernel corn if I cannot get fresh corn.) Cook until celery, onion and corn are done. Then add small "rivvels" made by mixing 2 cups of flour, 1 egg, and salt and pepper. Mix together until mixture is crumbly and then drop these into the broth and simmer about 15 minutes more. This soup can be simmered as long as you wish and seems to improve when reheated.

Martha Cramer

Ham Bone Soup

1 or more trimmed ham bones
6 quarts water
1 medium can tomatoes
1 teaspoon dried parsley
2 sprigs cut celery
3 peppercorns
2 tablespoons barley
3 cut carrots
   Half a small head of cabbage, cut up
   Salt
2 large diced potatoes

Place ham bone in two-gallon pot, add water, tomatoes, parsley, celery, peppercorns, barley, carrots and salt to taste. Boil for 2 hours, add cabbage and potatoes and cook for another half-hour.

More carrots can be used, also more cabbage and a little catsup to improve the flavor. The ham bone does not need to be trimmed too much, as parts of ham add to the flavor of the soup.

Stanley R. Rempala

Autumn Soup

1 pound ground beef	1 cup chopped onions
4 cups hot water	1 cup cut up carrots
1 cup cut up celery	1 cup cut up potatoes
2 teaspoons salt	½ teaspoon pepper
1 teaspoon meat extract	1 bay leaf, pinch of basil
6 whole fresh tomatoes, stems removed	

Brown beef slowly in hot fat in a heavy skillet. Add onions and cook 5 minutes. Loosen meat from bottom of kettle. Add remaining ingredients, except tomatoes; bring to boil, cover and simmer 20 minutes. Add the tomatoes; simmer 10 minutes more.

Nutritious for dieters; add a hearty dessert for others. Serves 6.

Edith Borne

Peanut Butter Soup

3 tablespoons onion, minced
1 tablespoon butter
¼ cup peanut butter (chunky style)
1 can cream of chicken soup
1 soup can of water
¼ cup milk

Sauté onion in butter. Blend in peanut butter. Stir in soup, a little at a time to blend. Stir in water and milk. Heat but do not boil. Serves 3.

Maysie Newsom

Mormon Whole Meal Soup

1 tablespoon butter	1 cup corn
2 pounds ground beef	1 cup diced carrots
2 quarts hot water	2 cups shredded cabbage
2 cups diced potatoes	2 onions, diced
1 cup diced celery	1½ teaspoon salt
2 cups tomatoes	¼ cup rice

Melt butter, add meat and brown. Add water and bring to a full rolling boil. Add vegetables. Bring back to a boil. Add rice and seasonings. Simmer 1 to 1½ hours.

Leslie Epperson

Fruit Salad

1 pkg. vanilla pudding
1 pkg. orange or lemon tapioca pudding
1 can mandarin oranges
1 can pineapple chunks
1 banana sliced.

(You may substitute vanilla tapioca pudding and one heaping tablespoon of frozen concentrated orange juice in place of the orange or lemon tapioca pudding.)

Cook puddings together with 3 cups liquid. (Use liquids from canned fruits and add water to make remainder 3 cups.) Cool slightly then add fruits. Refrigerate.

Beverly J. Saleske

Maple Nut Salad

1½ cup crushed pineapple (#2 can)
    drained
  2 packages cream cheese
  ½ cup chopped dates
  ¼ cup maple syrup
  1 cup cream, whipped
  ½ cup chopped nuts

Fold all ingredients together, and set in refrigerator.

Velda Block

Georgia Nut Salad

Beat in a heavy saucepan, 2 eggs until foamy. Add ½ cup sugar and a scant ½ cup vinegar. Cook until thick, stirring slowly with a wooden spoon. Take from heat and beat until smooth, then let cool. When cool add 2 tablespoons of cream and beat again. Set aside and pare and dice about 6 large apples. Pour cooled sauce over apples then gently fold in 1 cup pecans. Serve at once.

"This delicious salad came from a gracious Georgia plantation. A family recipe traditional for their Christmas menu."

Mozelle Hotchkiss

Cherry Coke Salad

1 can (1 pound) bing cherries
1 can (1 pound, 4 ounces) crushed pineapple
1 large package (6 ounce) cherry gelatin
2 bottles (6½ ounces each) cola

Drain juice from fruit; add water if necessary to make 2 cups. Heat juice to boiling; add gelatin, stir until dissolved. Cool; add cola and fruit. Pour into 1½ quart mold. Chill until set. Serve with salad dressing, cream cheese dressing or whipped cream.

Florence Howard

Use a Variety of Salad Greens

Head lettuce   Leaf lettuce
Bibb lettuce   Boston lettuce

Romaine   Escarole   Watercress
         Celery lettuce
Curly endive   Spinach

Unusual Additions to Salads

Sliced water chestnuts
Tiny croutons browned in garlic butter
Chopped raw asparagus tips
Artichoke hearts
Crisp bacon
Sliced mushrooms
Ripe or stuffed sliced olives
Anchovies
Sliced hard-cooked eggs

Pink Applesauce Mold

Add a dash of salt and ⅓ cup red hots to 1 can applesauce. Heat slowly until red hots are melted. Add 1 package lemon gelatin, dissolve. Then add 1 small bottle of 7-Up. Mold. Good with ham.

Irene Moyle

Eggnog Holiday Salad

1 can (1 pound) fruit cocktail
2 envelopes plain gelatin
1 can (11 ounces) mandarin oranges,
    cut in half
1 cup flaked coconut
2½ cups dairy eggnog
    Dash of nutmeg

Drain fruit, saving juice. Soften gelatin in juice and melt over hot water. Combine with rest of ingredients. Turn into 5-cup mold and chill until firm.

"This is very good to serve from Thanksgiving to New Years when eggnog is available. Has a delicious taste. When serving at Christmastime, a few extra maraschino cherries cut in half may be added. The extra red color makes it look more festive."

Maysie Newsom

Crab Louis

Louis Dressing:

- ¼ cup chili sauce
- ½ pound sour cream
- ¼ cup finely chopped green pepper
- ¼ cup finely chopped green onion
- 1 cup mayonnaise
- 1 teaspoon lemon juice
- Salt to taste

Ingredients:

- 1 head lettuce
- 1 cup crabmeat (more if desired)
- 2 avocadoes
- 1 small can string beets
- 1 small can pitted olives
- 2 boiled eggs
- 2 tomatoes
  Use remaining green pepper and green onion from dressing. Cut the green pepper in thin strips and onion in bite-size pieces.

Cover plates with bite-size pieces of lettuce. Put remaining ingredients in desired arrangement on top of lettuce. Pour dressing over top, or serve to the side in a small pitcher.

Note: This dressing can be used on green salads if any is left over. Yield 6.

Suzanna C. Bascochea

Tuna Crunch Salad

- 1-6 ounce can tuna, drained
- ¼ cup chopped sweet pickles
- 1 tablespoon minced onion
- 1 to 2 tablespoons lemon juice
- ¾ cup salad dressing
- 1½ cups shredded cabbage
- 1¼ cups crushed potato chips

Combine first 5 ingredients. Cover and chill until ready to serve, then add cabbage and toss. Add 1 cup of crushed potato chips and toss. Heap in bowl and sprinkle remaining chips on top. Yield 5-6.

Ruth Lovaasen

Macaroni-Ham Salad

- 2 cups cooked and cooled macaroni (Remember — use ½ amount uncooked)
- 1 cup diced cucumber
- 1 cup diced ham
- 1 tablespoon grated onion
- 1 tablespoon minced parsley
- ¾ cup mayonnaise
- ½ teaspoon salt
- ¼ teaspoon pepper

Combine all ingredients. Toss together until blended. Put in tomato cups and sprinkle with grated cheese. 4-6 servings.

Mary Reiner

Hearty Lunch Salad

- 1 cup carrots grated
- 2 tablespoons minced onion
- ½ cup diced celery
- ½ cup salad dressing
- 2 tablespoons cream or milk
- 2 tablespoons salad mustard
- 1 can salmon
- 1 can shoestring potatoes

Mix the first 7 ingredients together. Top salad with potatoes just before serving.

Frances Langbecker

Chinese Chicken Salad

- 4 cups cooked chicken (cut up)
- 1 can bamboo shoots (5 ounces, drained)
- 1 can water chestnuts (5 ounces, drained)
- 2 cans mandarin oranges (drained)
- 1 cup slivered almonds
- 2 tablespoons dehydrated onions (minced)
- 2 cups mayonnaise
- 2 cans Chinese noodles

Combine first 7 ingredients and chill. Serve on the Chinese noodles. Yield 6-8.

Mrs. Robert C. Sauer

Holiday Relish

1 package whole cranberries, raw
2 apples (unpeeled)
2 oranges (unpeeled)
1 small can crushed pineapple
1 cup chopped pecans
2¾ cups sugar
1 teaspoon red food coloring

Place cranberries and 2 cups of water in blender. Chop finely and drain. Place cored and quartered apples (unpeeled) and 2 cups water in blender. Chop finely and drain. Quarter oranges (unpeeled), remove seeds, and chop finely in blender. Do not add water. Use only juice from oranges. Mix all ingredients together in glass bowl and refrigerate overnight to enhance flavor. Yields approximately 1½ quarts

LaVada Whiteley

Rosy Applesauce Relish

1 #2 can applesauce
½ cup diced celery
½ cup (or less) raisins
½ cup red-hot cinnamon candies
2 teaspoons of prepared horseradish
(about, or to taste)

Combine and stir. Chill in refrigerator overnight. Stir before serving. Keeps well. Yield 4 cups.

Mrs. Don L. Jacobs

Quick Pickled Beets

1 #2 can or jar sliced beets
¼ cup vinegar
1 teaspoon salt
¼ teaspoon cinnamon
⅛ teaspoon cloves
Dash of pepper

Drain juice from beets. Add remaining ingredients to juice and bring to boiling. Pour over beets and sprinkle caraway seeds over top. Chill overnight.

Harriet Myles

Russian Dill Pickles

1 cup water
2 cups vinegar
1½ cups sugar
Cook to boiling.

Select thin cucumbers about 5 inches long. Wash and cut lengthwise in quarters. Put 1 head of dill, 1 small red pepper, ½ teaspoon salt and 2 teaspoons of mixed spice in each quart jar. Pack cucumbers in jars and pour hot liquid over cucumbers. Seal jars.

Edith Shaska

Sweet Dill Pickles

1 quart dill pickle chips
2 cups sugar
½ cup tarragon or apple cider vinegar
1 teaspoon celery seed
1 teaspoon mustard seed (optional)

Rinse and drain cucumber chips. Mix all other ingredients and bring to a boil. Remove from stove, let cool 10 minutes. Pack chips into jars and pour syrup over them. Seal jars and let set about a week.

Mrs. C. E. Mathews

Spiced Peaches

7 cups sugar
1 pint cider vinegar
1 pint water
Boil together for 20 minutes.

Add peeled fruit and boil until tender. To each jar add 3 whole cloves and 3 small sticks cinnamon. Fill jars with fruit. Cover with syrup and seal. This is enough for 6 quarts. Process for 20 minutes in canner in hot water bath.

This recipe can be used for spicing pears, watermelon rind, apricots and pineapples. The juice from spiced fruit is good for seasoning ham or pork.

Mrs. Chester A. Cramer

Potato Soufflé

4 tablespoons chopped onion
3 tablespoons melted butter
1 cup milk
2 tablespoons flour
   Salt and pepper
2 eggs separated
3 cups leftover mashed potatoes

Brown onion in butter, add flour and then milk. Add yolks and sauce to potatoes and mix well. Then fold in beaten egg whites. Bake in greased oven dish about 25 or 30 minutes at 350°F.

Mrs. Hugh Morenz

Green Beans, Cream Style

1-10 ounce package frozen green beans
1-3 ounce package cream cheese, softened
1 tablespoon milk
¼ teaspoon celery seed
¼ teaspoon salt

Cook beans according to package directions, drain.

Combine remaining ingredients, blend thoroughly. Add to beans to heat through. 4 servings.

Mrs. John Allen

Vegetable Platter Combinations

1. Pile whole kernel corn with green pepper in center of platter; surround with broiled tomato halves.
2. Mound of mashed squash surrounded with baked potatoes and buttered asparagus, topped with grated cheese.
3. Cauliflower head with buttered almonds, surrounded with glazed sweet potatoes and creamed green beans.
4. Buttered green lima beans surrounded by small creamed onions and glazed carrots.
5. Baked acorn squash halves filled with pineapple and brown sugar.
6. Broccoli spears topped with toasted almonds, surrounded with buttered whole kernel corn.

Beets Royale

1 #2 can pineapple chunks
2 tablespoons cornstarch
1 #3 can diced beets or can
    of very small beets
1 tablespoon vinegar
¾ teaspoon salt

Blend cornstarch with ½ cup pineapple juice. Add beet juice and cook until thickened. Add vinegar, salt, and pineapple and beets. Heat thoroughly.

Mrs. C. F. Frederick

Elegant Corn

1-16 ounce can corn
1 cup cracker crumbs
⅓ cup diced celery
¼ cup onion
¾ cup American cheese, cut
    in small pieces
1 teaspoon salt
2 eggs, well-beaten
2 tablespoons melted butter
¼ teaspoon paprika
1 cup milk

Combine all the ingredients and pour into a greased casserole. Bake in 350° oven for 50 minutes. 4-6 servings.

Mrs. Walter Weichert

Swedish Red Cabbage

1 medium head red cabbage, sliced
¼ cup butter
3 tablespoons brown sugar
¼ cup chopped onion
2 firm tart apples, sliced
2 tablespoons vinegar
½ teaspoon caraway seeds
½ teaspoon salt
¼ teaspoon pepper
½ cup grape juice

Sauté cabbage in butter for about 5 minutes, stirring occasionally. Add brown sugar, onions and apples; continue cooking for another 5 minutes. Add remaining ingredients; cover and simmer slowly for 30 or 35 minutes, stirring occasionally. Serve hot with meat course.

Mina Morris Scott

Scalloped Cabbage

1 small head cabbage
½ soup can milk
1 cup bread crumbs
1 can cream of chicken
    soup
½ cup grated cheese
Butter for topping

Cut cabbage in small wedges. Cook in salted water until tender. Drain thoroughly. Into greased casserole place alternate layers of cabbage and soup-milk-cheese mixture. Top with bread crumbs and dot generously with butter. Bake about 30 minutes at 350°. Yield 4-6 servings.

Mrs. Claud J. Mustain

Eggplant, Pizza Style

1 medium eggplant
1 beaten egg
⅓ cup fine dry bread crumbs
    Salad or olive oil
    Salt, pepper
1-8 ounce can (1 cup)
    seasoned tomato sauce
1 teaspoon oregano
2 tablespoons chopped parsley
¼ cup grated Parmesan cheese
4 to 6 slices (about 6 ounces)
    Mozzarella cheese

Pare eggplant, cut in ½ inch slices. Dip in beaten egg, then coat well with bread crumbs; let dry a few minutes. Brown lightly on both sides in hot oil. Overlap slices in a lightly buttered 10 x 6 x 1½ inch baking dish. Then sprinkle with salt, pepper, oregano, parsley and Parmesan cheese. Top with Mozzarella cheese. Pour tomato sauce over all. Bake in moderate oven (350°) for 20 minutes or until sauce is bubbly and cheese melts. Makes 5 or 6 servings.

Alberta Dredla

# CASSEROLES

String Bean Casserole

2 medium cans string beans
1 medium can Chinese vegetables
1 can condensed cream of mushroom soup
1 medium can French fried onion rings
1 cup grated cheddar cheese

Drain beans and vegetables. Add condensed soup as it comes from can (do not add water.) Top with fried onion rings. Bake for 25 minutes at 325°. Sprinkle cheese over top and bake an additional 5 minutes. Add salt and pepper to taste.

Stephanie Meisch

Recipe for a Good Day

Take two parts UNSELFISHNESS and one part of PATIENCE and work together. Add plenty of INDUSTRY. Lighten with good spirits and sweeten with KINDNESS. Put in SMILES as thick as raisins in plum pudding and bake by the warmth which steams from a LOVING HEART. If this fails to make a good day, the fault is not with the recipe but with the cook.

submitted by Mrs. V. M. Miller

Asparagus Almondine

1 can cream of chicken soup
¼ cup of milk
3 hard-cooked eggs cut in
    ⅛ inch thick slices
1 cup cubed American cheese
1 package frozen cut asparagus
1 cup sliced almonds
½ cup bread crumbs
2 tablespoons butter

Combine milk and soup. Stir in eggs, cheese and asparagus (which has been cooked until tender). Turn mixture into buttered casserole. Cover top with almonds, then crumbs. Dot with butter. Bake at 350° for 30 to 40 minutes, until bubbly and slightly brown on top.

Marian Butterbaugh

Yuletide Scalloped Onions

2 pounds small white onions
¼ cup butter or margarine
¼ cup flour
2 cups milk
½ teaspoon salt
¼ teaspoon pepper
1 cup grated sharp cheese
¼ cup chopped pimiento
¼ cup chopped parsley
½ cup bread crumbs

Peel onions, cook in salted water 15 minutes until just tender; drain. Place in baking dish.

Melt butter, add flour and blend until smooth, cook 3 minutes.

Heat milk, add to flour mixture slowly, stirring. Bring just to boil and cook about 5 minutes, stirring constantly with wire whip. Add salt and pepper.

Stir in cheese until melted; add pimiento and parsley, mix. Pour over onions. Mix crumbs with 1 tablespoon softened butter. Sprinkle as a border for pan. Brown in moderate oven (375°) for 15 minutes. Serves 8.

Florence W. Furgasan

Carrot Ring

¼ cup butter 3 eggs, separated
2 tablespoons flour 2 cups cooked carrots,
½ teaspoon salt   mashed and
⅛ teaspoon pepper   seasoned

Melt butter, add flour and seasoning. Add to slightly beaten egg yolks and blend smooth. Add cooled mashed carrots and mix well. Fold in stiffly beaten egg whites. Pour mixture into well-greased 1½ quart mold. Set mold in pan of hot water and bake ½ hour at 350°F oven.

Invert on large platter and fill center with buttered peas. Yield 8 servings.

Gladys Long

Lima Bean Supreme

1 pound lima beans, soak overnight. Drain, add water and boil 45 minutes, drain again.

Mix in baking dish:
    Beans
  1/2 pound butter
  1/2 cup brown sugar
   1 tablespoon dry mustard
  1/2 pint sour cream
   1 teaspoon molasses

Bake 1 hour at 350°. Stir once during baking time. Yield—6 servings.

Arline Quier

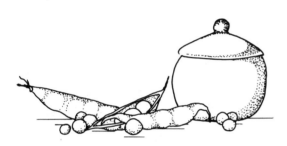

Barbecued Kraut

  4 strips bacon
1/2 onion diced
1/2 cup brown sugar
  1 #2 can tomatoes
    A-1 meat sauce
    Worcestershire sauce
    Barbecue sauce
  2 #2 cans chopped kraut

Dice and brown bacon. Drain off excess grease and add onion, brown slightly. Add brown sugar and tomatoes and let simmer for 15 minutes. Add a dash of A-1 meat sauce, Worcestershire sauce and barbecue sauce to above. Drain sauerkraut and place in baking dish. Add cooked mixture. Toss lightly. Bake 1 hour at 350°. Serves 6.

Willabelle L. Wiley

Chicken and Yams

  6 chicken breasts or 1 cut up fryer
1/4 cup flour   1/4 teaspoon salt
1/4 teaspoon paprika   Dash pepper
1/4 cup oil
1/2 cup cut up celery and leaves
  1 green bell pepper, sliced
  1 medium clove garlic or garlic salt
1/8 teaspoon thyme   Dash rosemary
  1 bay leaf
  1 can condensed mushroom soup
1/2 cup liquid added to soup (use wine, broth, or water)
  1 can whole white onions, drained
  6 medium sweet potatoes cooked, or 1 can

Dust chicken with flour, salt, paprika, and pepper. Lightly brown in oil, then arrange in large casserole or pan.

Add to drippings celery, green pepper, garlic, bay leaf and rosemary.

Cook about 5 minutes, stir in remaining seasoned flour, gradually blend in soup and liquid.

Arrange onions and sweet potatoes around chicken in casserole. Pour seasoned soup over all.

Cover and bake at 375° about 30 minutes, then uncover and bake 30 minutes longer.

Marian Hunter

Helen's Vegetable Casserole

  2 cups cooked carrots
  2 cups green beans
  2 cups celery
1/2 cup onions
1/2 cup green pepper
  1 can tomatoes
  4 teaspoons tapioca
  1 teaspoon sugar
    Salt and pepper

Bake 2 hours at 350°
Makes 6 to 8 servings.

Helen Williams

Macaroni Mousse

Heat together ½ cup milk and 2 table-spoons butter. Add 6 slices white bread cut into ½-inch squares (remove crusts).

1 cup cut up cheese	2 cups cooked
½ can pimiento (cut up)	elbow macaroni
½ medium green	
pepper (cut up)	2 eggs beaten
1 tablespoon minced onion	Salt to taste

Place in buttered casserole. Sprinkle crushed cornflakes and paprika on top and dot with butter or margarine. Bake in 300° oven for ¾ hour. Serves 7.

Sauce for mousse

Mix together:
- 2 tablespoons butter
- 2 tablespoons flour
- 2 cups milk

Cook and add 1 can shrimp, lobster or salmon.

Mrs. Wallace W. Morse

Baked Seafood Salad

½ cup chopped green pepper
¼ cup finely minced onion
1 cup chopped celery
1 cup cooked or canned crabmeat
1 cup cooked or canned shrimp
1 cup mayonnaise
½ teaspoon salt
1 teaspoon Worcestershire sauce
2 cups cornflakes crushed or
    1 cup dry bread crumbs
    Paprika
2 tablespoons butter

Combine green pepper, onion, celery, crabmeat, shrimps, mayonnaise, salt and Worcestershire and mix lightly. (If using canned seafood, rinse shrimps well in plenty of cold water and drain. Look crab-meat over for shell bits.)

Place mixture in individual shells or a shallow baking dish. Sprinkle with crumbs and dot with bits of butter. Bake at 350° for 30 minutes. Serve with lemon wedges. Serves 6 or 8.

Mrs. J. Davidson

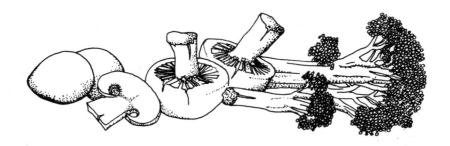

Yummy Casserole

1 can chow mein noodles
1 can cream of mushroom soup
1 cup shredded turkey or chicken
½ cup water
1 small can salted cashews
1 teaspoon grated onion
1 cup celery, cut fine

(Reserve ½ cup noodles for top.) Mix together and add noodles over top. Bake at 325° for 40 minutes.

Louise Hanicker

Rice Casserole

Use with a main meal dish instead of potatoes.
1 can beef consommé
1 can French onion soup
⅓ cup Parmesan cheese
1 cup (8 ounce can) mushrooms and juice
¼ pound butter
1½ cups raw converted rice

Bake 1 hour at 350°. Stir every 20 minutes. Yield 6 servings.

Audrey Mondloch

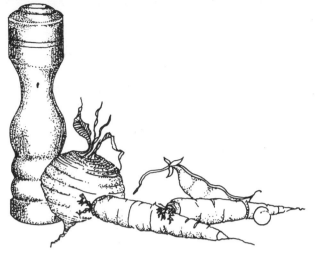

Quickie

1 can chicken rice soup
1 can cream of chicken soup
1 small can chicken
1 small can evaporated milk
1 small can mushrooms
1 small jar pimiento
1 can chow mein noodles

Mix and put in casserole. Top
with crushed potato chips. Bake
1 hour at 350°.

Lois I. Typer

 # MAIN DISHES

Broccoli

6 whole chicken breasts
4-10 ounce packages frozen broccoli
2 cans cream of chicken soup
1½ cups mayonnaise
⅔ cup half-and-half (half milk, half cream)
1½ cups grated cheddar cheese
2 teaspoons lemon juice
¼ teaspoon curry powder
1 cup fine dry bread crumbs, buttered

Cook chicken and let cool in liquid. Bone and cut in strips. Cook broccoli only until crisp tender. Mix together mayonnaise, half-and-half, cheese, lemon juice, curry and chicken soup. Pour over chicken and broccoli. Cover with bread crumbs. Bake at 350° for 40 minutes.

Mrs. Walter Rentsch

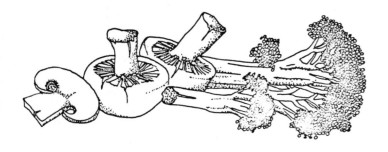

Cashew Beef

Brown in 1 tablespoon fat, 1 pound ground beef and 1 onion (minced). Add 1 can of cream of mushroom soup, 1 can cream of chicken soup and ½ cup milk, ¼ cup chopped green pepper, ½ cup chopped celery, 1 small can mushroom pieces, ½ cup cashew nuts, and 1 eight ounce package noodles cooked in boiling salted water and drained. Pour into greased casserole and top with potato chips or crumbs.

Bake 1½ hours at 350°F. Makes 10 servings.

Mrs. Lester V. Smith

Tuna Buffet

2 cans (6½ or 7 ounces each) tuna
    in vegetable oil
2 tablespoons finely chopped onions
1 cup sliced celery
1 medium green pepper, cut in strips
1 tablespoon curry powder
½ teaspoon ginger
1 teaspoon salt
1 can (14 ounces) pineapple chunks
1 can (10½ ounces) condensed cream
    of mushroom soup, undiluted
2 tablespoons raisins
1 tablespoon lemon juice
3 cups hot cooked rice

Drain oil from tuna into saucepan. Add onion, celery and green pepper, cook until crisp-tender. Stir in curry powder, ginger and salt. Drain syrup from pineapple and measure ½ cup. Add pineapple syrup, mushroom soup and raisins to saucepan. Bring mixture to boil, stirring constantly. Add lemon juice, pineapple and tuna. Heat to serving temperature. Serve with rice. Serves 6.

Mrs. D. C. Lemmon

Tamale Pie

Brown together:
    1 pound ground beef
    ½ pound salt pork, ground
    1 large onion, chopped
Add:
    1 large can tomatoes
    1 large can cream-style corn
    ½ cup olive oil

Cook slowly 10 minutes. In a separate pan heat 2 cups milk and add slowly 1½ cups yellow cornmeal. Stir until thick, then add:
    2 beaten eggs
    1 tablespoon salt
    1 tablespoon chili powder

Mix together with meat and add 1 can pitted ripe olives. Bake in a large casserole for 1 to 1½ hours. Serves at least 6. 300°

Mrs. John Bugbee

El Dorado

1 bag corn chips (medium size)
1 pound ground beef, browned
2 tablespoons onion, chopped
½ teaspoon garlic
2 cans tomato sauce (small)
    Mix last four ingredients together.
1 cup cottage cheese
1 cup sour cream
1 cup sliced olives
1 can Ortega chilies (diced)
    Mix last four ingredients together.

In oiled casserole place layer of chips, layer of meat mix, layer of cottage cheese mix. Sprinkle with grated cheese. Repeat layers and bake at 350°F. for 40 minutes.

Leila Teter

Contents of Cans

Size	Average Contents
#300	1¾ cups
1 tall	2 cups
303	2 cups
2	2½ cups
2½	3½ cups
3	4 cups
10	12-13 cups

Gourmet Omelet

8 garden onions   9 eggs
½ cup grated mellow cheese   ¼ cup milk
⅛ teaspoon salt   ⅛ teaspoon paprika
    ¼ cup melted butter or margarine

Cut onions finely, including green tops. Place in skillet with the heated butter or margarine. Cover with hot water, and cook slowly over medium heat until water is cooked out. Let onions brown slightly. Whip eggs until light, mix in cheese, add milk. Pour over the onions, and scramble. Serve with toast wedges. Serves 6. May be dusted with pepper instead of paprika if preferred.

Virginia K. Oliver

Yorkshire Hot Pot

4 shoulder lamb chops   2 teaspoons salt
1 garlic clove, minced   Pepper
4 small whole onions   1 can cream of mushroom soup
4 medium potatoes, halved, ½ can water
    pared   Paprika
1 package frozen cut beans
¼-½ teaspoon ground cloves

1. Brown chops in heavy skillet with garlic. Tuck onions and potatoes around and under chops. Add beans, cloves, salt, pepper, soup and water.
2. Cover, cook slowly 1 hour. Thicken and sprinkle with paprika.

Mrs. H. Kunnemann

St. Paul's Rice

1 pound bulk sausage   1 cup regular uncooked rice
1 bell pepper, chopped fine 4½ cups water
1 onion, chopped   ½ cup slivered almonds
1 cup chopped celery   Chopped parsley
1 package instant chicken noodle soup

Cook sausage in skillet, stirring through and cutting up to break into small bits. Drain off excess grease. Remove sausage. Sauté onion, pepper and celery. Mix the soup in water. Add rice and cook for seven minutes. Mix all ingredients together and put in a large baking dish; sprinkle almonds on top. Bake at 300° for 1 hour. Remove from oven and sprinkle a border of chopped parsley around the edge just before serving. Serves 4.

Fay Broyhill Edmonds

Veal Almondine

2 tablespoons butter
2 cups chicken stock or bouillon
2 tablespoons cornstarch
½ cup pineapple syrup
2 cups cubed cooked veal
½ cup drained canned crushed pineapple
½ cup toasted slivered almonds
½ cup chopped celery
1½ teaspoon salt.

Melt butter, add stock or bouillon, bring to a boil and reduce heat. Blend cornstarch and pineapple syrup and add to stock mixture until thickened. Boil 2 minutes. Add veal, pineapple, almonds, celery and salt. Heat thoroughly. Serve over chow mein noodles. 6 servings.

Mrs. Steven Frame

Spareribs With Caraway Kraut

2½ to 3 pounds spareribs, cut in pieces
2 teaspoons salt
¼ teaspoon pepper
1 #2½ can (3½ cups) sauerkraut
2 medium carrots, shredded
1½ cups tomato juice
2 tablespoons brown sugar
2 to 3 teaspoons caraway seed
1 unpared apple, finely chopped

Season ribs with salt and pepper. Combine kraut (including liquid) with remaining ingredients; place in Dutch oven. Place ribs, meaty side up, atop kraut. Bake, covered, in 350° oven 2½ to 3½ hours or until ribs are done, basting kraut with juices several times during the last hour. Makes 6 servings.

Nancy Watts

Swiss Steak in Sour Cream

Dredge round steak with flour, season with salt and pepper. Brown well on both sides in hot shortening. Add 2 sliced onions, 1 cup of sour cream (commercial), ½ cup grated cheese. Sprinkle paprika over all. Cover pan tightly and let simmer 2 hours at 300°.

Mrs. David Gruis

Hearty Ham Supper

2 cups cubed cooked ham
1 can whole kernel corn (drain)
1 cup diced cooked potatoes
¼ cup minced parsley
1 tablespoon finely chopped onion
¼ teaspoon paprika
¼ cup butter or margarine
¼ cup flour
2 cups milk
1 cup shredded American cheese

Make sauce of butter, flour and milk. Combine other ingredients in baking dish. Pour sauce over ham mixture and top with cheese. Bake 350° for ½ hour. 4-6 servings.

Iris Garrison

Wanted . . . Time

Grace Allard Morse

Time to have my close friends in
    to drink a cup of tea;
Time to read the book of verse
    my sister sent to me.
Time to sort my linens out
    and stack them in neat rows;
Time to look my scrapbook o'er
    and work with rhyme and prose.
Time to bake some muffins
    for the boy who mows our lawn;
Time to listen to the lark
    at morning's early dawn.
Time to cut pink roses
    for a neighbor living near;
Time to plan the garden
    I have wanted for a year.
Time to breakfast leisurely
    and scan the paper through . . .
Time, just to do the things
    I really want to do.

*Our sincere thanks to the author
whose address we were unable to locate.*

Stuffed Green Peppers

6 green peppers

Stuffing:

1½ to 2 pounds ground meat
½ cup grated onions
1 cup raw rice
½ cup finely chopped celery
3 eggs
1 teaspoon salt
1 tablespoon fresh-ground pepper
½ cup bread crumbs
1 cup tomato juice and milk to make quite moist

Sauce:

4 cups tomato soup
1 cup tomato juice
1 can tomato sauce

Remove tops, membranes and seeds from peppers. Mix all ingredients for stuffing and fill peppers. If any mixture remains form into 2 inch balls and place all in baking dish or small roaster pan. Cover with sauce. Spoon sauce over peppers during baking period. Bake 2½ hours at 325°. Serves 6-8.

Arlene Steelman   23

CHICKEN

Parmesan Chicken

1 frying chicken (cut up)
2 eggs well beaten with 2 tablespoons water
1½ cups cornflake crumbs
½ cup grated Parmesan cheese
1½ teaspoons salt
1 teaspoon onion salt
1 cup butter

Rinse chicken and pat dry. Dip in egg and water mixture. Combine crumbs with cheese, salt and onion salt. Drain chicken and coat heavily with the crumb mixture. Place in a foil lined pan which has been coated with half of the butter. Dot chicken with the remaining butter. Cover over with foil. Bake in a preheated oven 375° for 1 hour or until crisp and tender.

Mrs. Vernon Harter

Chicken Newburg

⅓ cup butter
¼ cup flour
2 cups milk
¾ cup shredded cheddar cheese
1 tablespoon chopped pimiento
1 teaspoon salt
½ cup toasted slivered almonds
½ cup sliced fresh mushrooms
1½ cups cooked sliced chicken
¼ cup cooking sherry
1 teaspoon minced onion
¼ teaspoon pepper

Melt butter and sauté mushrooms for 2 minutes in chafing dish. Stir in flour until smooth. Add milk, stirring constantly. Add chicken and all other ingredients except almonds. Top with almonds just before serving. Serve with rice or patty shells.

Mitzie Turck

Broiled Chicken

Select broiler chicken (1½ to 2 pounds). Split lengthwise. Brush with melted butter and season with salt and pepper.

Broil slowly, skin side down, about 8 inches from heat. Turn every 15 minutes, brushing each time with butter and lemon juice.

Broil 45 to 60 minutes or until nicely browned.

Mrs. James Turner

Roast Chicken

Select roasting chicken. Wash and pat dry. Sprinkle 1 teaspoon salt inside cavity. Stuffing may be made ahead of time but never placed in chicken until time for roasting. Make 1 cup stuffing for each ready to cook pound of chicken. Stuff body and neck cavities lightly. Close cavity with a skewer and string. Rub skin with chicken fat. Place breast side up in shallow roasting pan. Insert meat thermometer so that bulb is in the center of the inside thigh muscle. A thin cloth moistened with melted fat may be placed over chicken to help uniform browning. Keep cloth moist with fat in pan. Roast at 325° until meat thermometer registers 190°-200°

Stuffing:
Ingredients for 5 pound chicken

½ cup butter
½ cup chopped onion
½ cup chopped celery
4 cups dry bread cubes
1 tablespoon minced parsley
1 teaspoon salt
⅛ teaspoon pepper

Sauté onions and celery in butter until tender. Add other ingredients and toss lightly. Add bouillon, stock or water if moist stuffing is desired (stock made from cooking giblets).

Mrs. Boris Zielinski

Party Chicken

4 whole chicken breasts (boned)
8 slices of bacon
1 4-ounce jar of dried beef
1 cup sour cream
1 can mushroom soup

Separate beef and place in a layer on bottom of a greased 8-inch square pan. Wrap bacon around chicken breasts and lay on beef slices. Mix undiluted soup and sour cream. Pour over chicken breasts. Refrigerate overnight. Bake at 350° for 2 hours.

Bea White

Yugoslavian Paprikash

¼ cup butter
1 frying chicken (cut up)
½ cup chopped onion
¼ cup flour
2 tablespoons paprika
2 teaspoons salt
¼ teaspoon pepper
1 can chicken broth
2 cups sour cream
1 tablespoon Worcestershire sauce
1-8 ounce package medium noodles
    cooked and drained.

Melt butter in large frypan. Sauté chicken until lightly brown. Remove chicken, add onion. Blend in flour, paprika, salt and pepper. Add chicken broth and cook, stirring constantly until thick and smooth. Stir in sour cream and Worcestershire sauce.

Mix ½ of sauce with cooked noodles and pour into 3 quart baking dish. Arrange chicken on top of noodle mixture and pour remaining sauce over chicken. Bake at 325° for 1 hour. 6 servings.

Mary Novak

Baked Chicken

4 cups diced cooked chicken
¾ cup mayonnaise
¾ cup canned cream of chicken soup
2 cups chopped celery
4 hard-cooked eggs, sliced
1 teaspoon salt
1 teaspoon finely minced onion
2 tablespoons lemon juice
2 pimientos, cut up
1 cup crushed potato chips
⅔ cup finely shredded sharp cheddar
⅓ cup chopped almonds

Mix first 9 ingredients. Put in large shallow 1½ quart baking dish. Combine potato chips with cheese and almonds and sprinkle on top. Chill several hours or overnight. Bake in hot oven (400° F.) 25 minutes, or until heated.

Mrs. Leo Waters

Chicken Creole

1 stewing chicken (5-6 pounds)
1 cup chopped celery
2 green peppers, chopped
2 onions, chopped
½ pound thin spaghetti, broken
1 tablespoon Worcestershire sauce
1 can pimiento, chopped
1 can mushrooms, chopped
1 pound American cheese
Salt and pepper to taste

Boil chicken until very tender. Remove from broth, (about 2 quarts broth needed). Boil celery, peppers and onions in broth for 20 minutes. Add broken spaghetti, and boil 20 more minutes. Then add Worcestershire sauce, salt and pepper, pimientos and mushrooms. Dice chicken; and add to above. Grate cheese and mix well in above mixture. Put in baking dishes and leave in refrigerator for 24 hours. Just before serving time, place in 400° oven until warmed all through, at least ½ hour. Serves 10.

Lucille Pearce

Orange-Glazed Rack of Lamb

1 rib rack of lamb
½ cup orange marmalade
1 tablespoon brown sugar
2 teaspoons prepared mustard
3 tablespoons lemon juice
  Orange slices and maraschino cherries
    for garnish

Place lamb on rack in roasting pan. Roast in 350° oven 1¼ hours, or until meat thermometer registers 175 to 180°. Meanwhile combine marmalade, brown sugar, mustard and lemon juice in small saucepan and heat, stirring constantly until blended. Baste lamb with mixture during last half hour. Garnish with orange slices and cherries.

Gladys Biesik

Greek Meat Loaf

½ cup chopped onion
2 tablespoons butter
½ cup shredded carrot
½ cup shredded raw potato
1 small eggplant (about 1 pound) trimmed, pared and shredded (About 2½ cups)
2 cloves of garlic, thinly sliced
2 pounds meat loaf mixture (beef, veal, pork)
2 eggs

2 medium size tomatoes, peeled and finely diced (1 cup)
1½ cups fine dry bread crumbs
3 teaspoons salt
½ teaspoon ground cinnamon
¼ teaspoon pepper
4 tablespoons lemon juice
2 tablespoons sugar

Sauté onion in butter or margarine in a medium size skillet, remove from heat; stir in carrot, potato, eggplant, and garlic, tossing to coat well. Cover. Cook 5 minutes or until wilted but still crisp.

Combine meat loaf mixture, eggs, tomatoes, bread crumbs, salt, cinnamon, pepper, 2 tablespoons of lemon juice and the cooked vegetables in a large bowl, mixing lightly. Form into loaf and put into a lightly greased shallow baking pan.

Bake in moderate oven (350°) for 45 minutes. Mix remaining 2 tablespoons of lemon juice and sugar in a cup, stirring until sugar is dissolved. Brush over loaf. Continue to bake 15 minutes longer, or until brown and glazed. Lift to heated platter with 2 wide spatulas. 8 servings.

Mrs. Nick Costas

Barbecue Sauce

Suitable for any kind of meat or fowl. Brush on with a pastry brush as the meat is cooking.

1 pint cider vinegar
½ cup salt
1¼ cup granulated sugar
1 teaspoon celery seed
1 tablespoon red pepper
2 tablespoons black pepper
Unstrained juice and pulp of 4 lemons
1 large grated onion

Mix all ingredients. Bring to boil in saucepan. Remove immediately from fire (do not overcook) and cool. Store mixture in a covered quart jar and let season for at least a week, occasionally shaking the jar. No need to store in refrigerator. It will keep perfectly on the pantry shelf.

Beatrice Branch

Veal Cutlets Cordon Bleu

12 veal cutlets
Pepper
6 slices swiss cheese
6 slices boiled ham
½ cup flour
¼ teaspoon nutmeg
¼ teaspoon cloves (ground)
3 eggs, beaten
1 cup dry bread crumbs
¾ cup butter

Pound veal. Sprinkle with salt and pepper. Place 1 slice of cheese and 1 slice of ham on each patty. Cover with remaining patties. Roll in flour and spice mixture, dip in eggs and then into crumbs. Brown 5 minutes on each side. White sauce with mushrooms may be poured over before serving.

Mrs. Harvey Knoll

Pepper Steak

1½ pounds boneless round steak
1 garlic clove, minced
2 large tomatoes, skinned
    and chopped
4 medium green peppers,
    seeded and cut into strips

¼ teaspoon ground black pepper
1¼ teaspoons ground ginger
¼ cup olive oil
¼ cup soy sauce
½ teaspoon sugar
1¼ cups beef bouillon or stock
2 tablespoons cornstarch

Cut meat across the grain into thin strips. Heat the oil and brown the meat and garlic in it quickly. Then stir in tomatoes and peppers. Add soy sauce, pepper, sugar, ginger and ¾ cup of stock. Cover and cook 20 minutes or until meat strips are tender. Blend cornstarch with remaining stock. Stir into meat mixture, bring to boil and simmer for two minutes, stirring constantly. Serve over bed of rice.

Ruth Guidi

Swedish Glottstek

4 pounds rolled beef chuck
1 tablespoon salt
½ teaspoon allspice
½ teaspoon pepper
4 tablespoons butter
1 tablespoon oil
2 large onions, minced

1 teaspoon anchovy paste
2 bay leaves
2 tablespoons vinegar
2 tablespoons molasses
2 tablespoons flour
4 tablespoons water
½ cup heavy cream, whipped

Rub the salt, pepper and allspice on the meat and brown in the butter and oil. Add the onions, anchovy paste, bay leaf, vinegar and molasses. Cover and simmer 2 to 3 hours until meat is tender. Slice the meat thin and surround with vegetables. Make the gravy with flour dissolved in cold water then fold in the whipped cream. Serves 8.

Mrs. Peter Gaber

Crown-of-Gold Meat Loaf

1½ cups fine, soft bread crumbs
4 egg yolks
1½ teaspoons salt
1½ tablespoons prepared horseradish
2 tablespoons minced onion

1½ pounds ground lean
    chuck beef
2 tablespoons mustard
3 tablespoons finely diced
    green pepper
⅓ cup catsup

Topping:
4 egg whites
4 tablespoons mustard
¼ teaspoon cream of tartar

Mix bread crumbs with meat. Combine remaining ingredients. Blend into meat-bread mixture. Pack lightly into a 9-inch casserole and bake at 325° for 30 minutes. To make topping, beat egg whites until foamy; add cream of tartar and beat until very stiff. Fold into mustard gently. Swirl on hot meat. Return to oven and bake 20 to 25 minutes longer or until tipped with brown. Makes 6-8 servings.

Sister Mercedes SCC

Sauerbraten

1½ pounds beef cubes
1 tablespoon fat
1 envelope brown gravy mix
2 cups water
1 tablespoon minced onion
2 tablespoons white wine vinegar
2 tablespoons brown sugar
½ teaspoon salt
¼ teaspoon pepper
½ teaspoon ginger
1 teaspoon Worcestershire sauce
1 bay leaf
Hot buttered noodles

Cut meat into 1-inch pieces. Brown in hot fat. Remove from skillet. Add gravy and water to skillet and bring to boil, stirring constantly. Stir in remaining ingredients except noodles. Return meat to skillet and simmer 1½ hours. Stir occasionally. Remove bay leaf. Serve over hot, buttered noodles. Serves 6.

Faye Wheatley

Spanish Steak

1¼ pounds round steak
1 tablespoon vinegar
1 teaspoon salt
¼ teaspoon pepper
2 tablespoons chopped onion
1 tablespoon chopped parsley
2 tablespoons chopped celery leaves
½ cup chopped green pepper
1 #2 can tomatoes

Pound steak on both sides with edge of sturdy saucer. Cover with mixture of the remaining ingredients. Let stand for 1 hour. Lift meat out and drain. Save all of juice. Brown meat in 2 tablespoons meat drippings on both sides. Place in shallow baking dish and add tomato mixture in which meat was soaked. Cover. Bake 2 hours at 325°. Serves 6

Judy O'Connell

Roast Beef
(flavored with "trimmings"!)

Take vegetable trimmings that you usually throw out such as celery leaves, carrot peelings and ends, lettuce leaves (anything except vegetables with starch content). Line the bottom of the roast pan with them, using plenty of the trimmings. Place roast on top of this and put a piece of beef fat on top of the roast and put about half an inch of water in the pan to keep them moist. Place your roast in the oven in an uncovered pan. Roast in 300° oven. Baste the roast every half hour with juice from the bottom of the pan. If it evaporates, add water to the half-inch level. Continue with the basting until the roast is done.

Mrs. Wiley Seward

Lasagne

Brown together:

2 pounds ground beef
1 large onion, chopped
1 or two tablespoons olive oil
1 teaspoon Worcestershire sauce
  Garlic salt, salt, and pepper to taste

Add:

2 cans tomato sauce
1 can tomato paste
1 can tomatoes
1 teaspoon oregano
2 bay leaves

Simmer, covered, at least 2 hours or until cooked down. Stir often. Boil 1 package lasagne noodles, blanch, and drain. Grease a large 9 x 13-inch casserole. Mix 1 pint cottage cheese with 2 raw eggs. Place one layer noodles in casserole and cover with meat sauce; add ½ the cottage cheese mixture. Cover with grated Parmesan. Add a layer of Mozzarella or Provolone cheese. Repeat. Usually only about 2 layers are possible and it is best to end with the cheese on top. About 6 slices of Mozzarella or Provolone cheese are needed. Bake at 350° about 30 minutes or until cheese is melted and the sauce is bubbly.

Mrs. John H. Bugbee

Spice Sauce for Ham

2 tablespoons red wine garlic vinegar
2 tablespoons prepared mustard
½ teaspoon ground cloves
½ teaspoon cinnamon
1 cup apple jelly

Place ingredients in pan over low fire. Stir until jelly is smooth. Remove from fire. Sauce will jell when cold. Re-heat and serve over ham.

Mrs. W. S. McFarlane

Sour Cream Scalloped Potatoes and Ham

2 slices smoked ham (½ inch thick)
8 medium potatoes (sliced thin)
1 can cream of mushroom soup
1 cup sour cream
1 teaspoon salt
1 cup sliced onions
  Dash of pepper
1 cup shredded cheddar cheese.

Cut ham into 8 serving pieces. Slice potatoes. Combine soup, sour cream, salt and pepper. In greased 3 quart casserole alternate layers of ham, potatoes and onions with sour cream mixture. Top with shredded cheese. Cover casserole loosely with foil. Bake at 325° for 2½ hours. Yields 8 servings.

M. Neacy

Horseradish Dressing

Combine ½ teaspoon salt, ⅛ teaspoon white pepper, dash of cayenne pepper. Whip 1 cup heavy cream. Add seasonings to cream. Combine ½ teaspoon sugar, 2 tablespoons cider vinegar, ½ cup drained horseradish. Add this mixture to the seasoned cream.

Singapore Pork and Cabbage

(A one-dish meal)

1 pound pork shoulder, cut in strips or use leftover pork
2 quarts shredded cabbage
1 cup (8 ounce can) water chestnuts, drained, sliced
1 cup sliced mushrooms
2 tablespoons chopped pimiento
1 cup water
¾ cup Italian dressing
½ cup soy sauce
4 tablespoons cornstarch

If using raw pork, brown meat; cover and cook 15 minutes. Drain. If using leftover pork, slice and set aside while preparing vegetables. Mix vegetables, water, and Italian dressing; cook 8 to 10 minutes. Add meat, stir till heated. Add soy sauce combined with cornstarch; stir until thickened. Serve over rice, if desired. Makes 6 servings.

Evelyn L. Jenney

Crown Roast of Pork

Place crown roast of 16 ribs (about 4½ pounds) on rack in a shallow pan. Season the meat to your own tastes with salt and freshly ground pepper. Insert meat thermometer into the fleshiest part of the meat, making sure that it is not touching a bone. Cover exposed rib ends with foil. Place in 350° oven and cook for 1½ hours. Then remove it and fill the crown with your favorite stuffing. Return to oven for another hour or until the thermometer reads 185°. Serves 8.

Mrs. L. Bolerud

Stuffed Pork Chops

6 rib or loin chops, ¾ or more inches thick with pockets cut.
  Trim off excess fat. Prepare a dressing of:
1 cup bread crumbs
¼ cup chopped celery
¼ cup chopped onion
2 tablespoons chopped parsley
¼ teaspoon salt
⅛ teaspoon paprika
  Enough milk to moisten dressing

Fill pockets with dressing and sew together or fasten with toothpicks. Sear in hot skillet, then place in 9 x 13 inch baking dish. Dilute 1 can cream of mushroom soup with ⅓ can milk and cover the chops with the soup. Cover pan with foil and bake at 350° about 1 hour. Serves 6.

Mrs. John Bugbee

 # GAME

Game Notes

Duck, Goose, Venison:

To remove wild flavor soak birds for 3 hours in water to which 1 tablespoon baking soda and 1 tablespoon salt has been added.

Try to remove all shot pellets from flesh of birds so there is no chance of biting into one while eating cooked fowl.

It is very important that venison be cleaned immediately and that all meat is clear of any hair particles. Cut off excess tallow as this will give meat a strong flavor.

Wild Duck With Apple Raisin Stuffing

6 cups dry bread crumbs
1 cup cubed apple
½ cup raisins
¾ cup butter, melted
2 teaspoons salt
½ teaspoon pepper
¼ teaspoon cinnamon
⅛ teaspoon ginger
3 ducks

Clean ducks thoroughly. Combine other ingredients in bowl and mix. Fill cavity of ducks and close opening with skewers or string.

Place in roasting pan (breast side up) and roast for 15 minutes uncovered at 450°, reduce heat to 325°. Cover ducks and bake at least another 2 hours. Serves 6.

Doris Milligan

Venison Teriyaki Style

2 pound venison steak
⅓ cup soy sauce
1 tablespoon sugar
1 tablespoon minced onion
2 garlic cloves, crushed
½ teaspoon ginger
2 bay leaves
⅓ cup cooking oil

Cut meat into 6 equal pieces. Place in baking dish. Combine remaining ingredients and pour over venison. Cover and refrigerate overnight.

Drain. Place on broiler rack about 5 inches from heat. Broil 10 minutes brushing on marinade periodically. Turn steak and broil 5 minutes more. Serves 6.

Lisa Wainwright

Pheasant In Gourmet Sauce

2 pheasants	¼ cup shortening
½ cup flour	1 clove garlic, crushed
1 teaspoon salt	¼ cup chopped olives
1 teaspoon paprika	½ cup water
⅛ teaspoon pepper	½ teaspoon Worcestershire sauce
⅛ teaspoon sweet basil	½ cup white cooking wine

Clean pheasant well, removing all buckshot and pin feathers. Cut into serving pieces. Coat bird pieces with seasoned flour. Heat shortening in heavy skillet. Brown pheasant on all sides. Add garlic, olives, water and Worcestershire sauce. Cover and simmer 45 minutes. Turn pheasant and add wine. Recover and simmer another 45 minutes (longer if needed). Add additional water to make extra sauce.

Mrs. Bradford Williams

Hasenpfeffer

2½ pound rabbit, cut in pieces	1 onion sliced	⅓ cup flour
1¼ cups water	3 bay leaves	⅓ cup shortening
¾ cup vinegar	10 whole cloves	2 tablespoons brown sugar
	2 teaspoons salt	1 cup sour cream
	½ teaspoon pepper	

Place rabbit (make sure it is well cleaned) in bowl and cover with water, vinegar mixture. Add onion, bay leaves, cloves, 1 teaspoon salt and pepper. Cover tightly and refrigerate 3 days. (Hold liquid for further use.) Remove rabbit, roll in flour and remaining salt. Melt shortening in heavy skillet and fry rabbit until golden brown, turn frequently. Add slowly 1 cup strained vinegar mixture and brown sugar. Cover and simmer for 1 hour. Add sour cream just before serving.

Anna Schultz

Baked Fish With Lemon Mushroom Sauce

2 packages frozen haddock fillets
1 can undiluted cream of mushroom soup
½ cup milk
1 can sliced mushrooms
1 large onion, chopped
2 tablespoons lemon juice
1 teaspoon paprika
½ teaspoon salt
¼ teaspoon oregano
¼ teaspoon pepper
1 bay leaf, crushed

Place frozen fillets in shallow buttered baking dish. (9") In saucepan combine rest of ingredients. Simmer 10 minutes. Pour over fillets.

Top with 1 cup buttered crumbs lightly seasoned with poultry seasoning (or 1 cup prepared stuffing mix). Dot with butter. Bake 45 minutes at 375°. Serves 6. Recipe may be halved easily.

Mrs. Roger C. Wilder

Baked Ocean Perch

¼ cup flour
½ teaspoon salt
¼ teaspoon pepper

2 pounds ocean perch fillets
2 tablespoons butter
⅓ cup grated onion
3 tablespoon lemon juice
½ cup minced parsley
1 cup sour cream
½ cup shredded American cheese
¼ cup buttered bread crumbs

Dip fish in flour, salt and pepper mixture. Place in a buttered 12 x 8 inch baking dish.

Melt butter in saucepan, add onion and sauté until tender. Remove from heat, add lemon juice, parsley, sour cream and cheese. Spread over fish. Sprinkle with crumbs. Bake 375° for 30 to 40 minutes. Serves 6.

Jody Petry

Baked Stuffed Pike

2 to 3 pound dressed whole fish
Salt
2 cups stuffing
3 tablespoons melted butter for basting

Stuffing: Lemon Bread Stuffing

¼ cup butter
2 tablespoons grated onion
2 cups soft bread cubes (slightly moist prepared stuffing may be used. If so eliminate thyme in recipe).
2 tablespoons lemon juice
2 teaspoons grated lemon rind
¼ teaspoon thyme
¼ teaspoon salt
¼ teaspoon freshly ground pepper

Salt inside of fish. Melt butter for stuffing and sauté onions until tender. Add remaining ingredients.

Fill fish with stuffing securing edges with wooden picks. Place in shallow baking dish and brush with melted butter. Bake at 450° for 10 minutes. Reduce heat to 350° and continue baking for 30 to 40 minutes longer. Baste with butter during baking period. Remove picks and garnish with parsley and lemon wedges.

June Parson

Pan-fried Fish

2 pounds dressed fish pieces
½ cup milk
1 egg, slightly beaten
½ cup flour, cornmeal, pancake mix or cracker crumbs
¼ cup shortening
Salt
Pepper

Wash and dry fish. Dip in egg, milk mixture. Roll in dry ingredient used.

Salt and pepper to taste.

Heat shortening in heavy skillet. Fry fish about 5 to 7 minutes.

Turn fish only once and do not crowd in the pan. Serve with tartar sauce.

Marilyn Ross

# BREADS

Banana Nut Bread

2 cups sifted flour
2 teaspoons baking powder
1 teaspoon salt
½ teaspoon baking soda
1 cup sugar
½ cup butter or margarine
2 eggs
1 cup mashed bananas
1 teaspoon lemon juice
1 cup chopped nuts

Sift together flour, baking powder, salt, soda, and sugar. Add shortening, eggs, bananas and lemon juice. Stir to combine ingredients, then beat 2 minutes at medium speed on electric mixer or 300 strokes by hand. Stir in ¾ cup nuts. Pour into greased loaf pan 5¼ x 9½ inches. Sprinkle ¼ cup nuts over top of batter. Bake in moderate oven 350° degrees 1 hour and 15 minutes. Makes one loaf.

Ruth Sprenkle

Apple Bread

Cream together:

½ cup butter
1 cup white sugar
2 eggs
1 teaspoon vanilla
½ teaspoon salt
1 teaspoon soda dissolved in
    2 tablespoons sour milk

Add:

2 cups diced apples
2 cups sifted flour

Turn into 2 small or 1 large bread tin. Greased and floured.

Topping: Mix together

2 tablespoons butter
2 tablespoons flour
2 tablespoons sugar
1 teaspoon cinnamon

Sprinkle on top of loaf and bake 1 hour at 325°.

Mrs. Gordon A. Luscher

Cranberry Orange Bread

2 cups flour
1 cup sugar
1½ teaspoons baking powder
½ teaspoon salt
1 egg beaten
2 tablespoons shortening

Grated rind and juice of
1 orange plus water to
    make ¾ cup, or use
    ¾ cup orange juice.
1 cup raw cranberries,
    cut in halves

Measure flour and blend dry ingredients. Mix in shortening, orange rind and juice and egg. Fold in cranberries. Bake one hour at 350°F. in a well greased 9x5x3-inch loaf pan. Cool thoroughly before slicing.

James F. Bennett

Saffron Bread

2½ cups milk
½ pound butter
1 package saffron
1 teaspoon salt
1½ cups seeded raisins

2 cakes yeast
1 cup sugar
2 eggs
8 cups flour

Heat milk, add butter to melt and cool to lukewarm. Dissolve saffron and yeast in 1 teaspoon milk. Add to milk with the sugar—blend in beaten eggs. Stir in flour until sticky and knead in rest of flour along with raisins.

Keep kneading until smooth, firm and glossy. Let rise in greased bowl until double in size. Place on board and shape into braided loaves. Let rise one hour after placing in bread tins. Bake 375° for 45 minutes. Makes 2 loaves.

Jill Susan Dalbey

Sour Cream Graham Bread

2 eggs, well beaten
1½ cups maple syrup
½ cup thick sour cream
2 cups white flour

1½ cup sour milk
2 cups graham flour
1½ teaspoon salt
2 teaspoons soda
2 teaspoons baking powder

Sift dry ingredients together. Beat eggs well, stir into cream, milk and syrup. Beat in dry ingredients. Batter should be stiff. Add more graham flour if necessary. Butter bread tins and line with heavy waxed paper. Fill ⅔ full. Bake at 375° for 1 hour, reduce heat the last part of time. Test with a toothpick.

Donna Kingsley

White Bread

2 packages active dry yeast
½ cup warm water
⅓ cup sugar
⅓ cup shortening
2 tablespoons salt
2 cups milk, scalded
1½ cup cold water
10 to 12 cups all purpose flour

Soften yeast in warm water.

In large mixing bowl blend well sugar, shortening, salt and hot milk until shortening is melted. Add cold water, cool. Stir in yeast. Gradually add flour to make a stiff dough.

Knead on floured board until smooth (5 to 10 minutes). Place in greased bowl, turn dough so all sides are greased. Cover with damp towel. Let rise until double in size (about 2 to 2½ hours).

Punch down dough by plunging your fist in center of dough. Turn upside down in bowl and let rise another 30 minutes.

Place on floured board and divide in fourths. Mold into balls, cover and let rise 15 minutes more. Shape into loaves. Place in well-greased loaf pans. Cover with damp towel. Let rise until dough is well above pan edges (about 1½ to 2 hours).

Bake at 375° for 40 to 50 minutes.

Remove from pan onto wire rack to cool. Makes 4 loaves.

Marianne Morgan

A Cook's Prayer

Lord, guide my willing hands
To bake my bread today,
To mix a little laughter
In what I do or say.

Help me to feed my family
With good food seasoned right,
With wisdom of a loving heart
Keep my kitchen shining bright.

Guide my erring thoughts to Heaven
When my spirit is sad and low,
Help me set my dinner table
With food for hearts that glow.

Polly Perkins

Apricot Bread

2 cups sifted regular flour
2½ teaspoons baking powder
¾ teaspoon salt
¾ cup crunchy nut-like cereal
⅔ cup chopped dried apricots
1 cup sugar
1 egg
1¼ cup milk
2 tablespoons shortening, melted

Sift flour, sugar, baking powder and salt into large bowl; stir in cereal and apricots. Beat egg well with milk in a small bowl; stir in shortening. Add to flour mixture all at once; stir until evenly moist. Pour in a greased loaf pan 9 x 5 x 3 inches. Bake at 350° 1 hour and 5 minutes or until toothpick comes out clean. Store, wrapped, overnight.

Fern Snyder

Pumpkin Bread

3½ cups flour
3 cups sugar
2 teaspoons soda
1 teaspoon each
 cinnamon, salt, nutmeg
4 eggs
2 cups pumpkin (#303 can)
1 cup cooking oil
⅔ cup water
1 teaspoon vanilla
1 cup nuts

Mix flour, soda, sugar and spice together. Make a well or hole in dry ingredients and add pumpkin, eggs, oil, and water. Beat until smooth, add nuts and vanilla. Pour into greased loaf pans and bake 1 hour at 350°.

This will make two 4 x 9-inch loaf pans or two 2-pound coffee cans or four 1-pound coffee cans. Makes a moist bread and is easy to mail in the coffee cans, as it keeps fresh a long time.

Betty Johnson

Oatmeal Bread

1 cup uncooked oatmeal (quick)
1 cup milk, scalded
½ cup boiling water
⅓ cup shortening (bacon drippings are good)
½ cup brown sugar, firmly packed
2 teaspoons salt
2 packages dry yeast
½ cup warm water
5 cups sifted flour

Put oatmeal in large bowl, stir in milk and boiling water. Add shortening, sugar and salt. Let stand until lukewarm. Sprinkle yeast into ½ cup of warm water. Stir until dissolved. Stir into oatmeal mixture, add ½ the flour, mix until smooth. Add remaining flour, a little at a time. Mix until dough leaves side of bowl. Turn out on board and knead 7 minutes. Place dough in greased bowl. Cover with damp cloth and let rise 1½ hours. Knead and shape into loaves. Bake at 400° for 10 minutes. Reduce heat to 350°, bake 40 minutes. Makes 2 loaves.

Thelma E. King

Soybean Bread

2 cups of water or milk
2 cups of soybean flour
2 cups of white flour (approximately)
1 tablespoon of shortening
1 tablespoon of sugar
1 teaspoon of salt
1 cake yeast

Prepare soft dough according to the usual method, using the soybean flour. Then add enough white flour to mix to a consistency for kneading. Let rise until double in bulk, mix, and let rise again.

Make into loaves and place in a pan. When double in bulk, bake at 375°F. Due to the composition of soybean flour, the mixture requires more kneading, and rises more slowly than white bread. This recipe makes 2 small loaves.

Della C. Pigg

French Bread

2½ cups warm water
1 tablespoon sugar
1 tablespoon salt
1 package active
   dry yeast
2 tablespoons soft shortening
½ cup water
½ teaspoon salt
1½ teaspoons cornstarch
   Sesame seed
8½ cups sifted flour

Combine first four ingredients; stir to dissolve yeast; let stand 5 minutes. Stir in flour and shortening, then work flour in with hands. Knead until smooth and elastic. Cover; let rise in warm place until doubled. Shape into 3 balls. Let rest 15 minutes. Shape each ball into a roll 15 inches long, tapered at each end. Place on baking sheet, cover with a towel; let rise until light. Meanwhile combine water, remaining salt and cornstarch. Cook and stir until thickened and clear. Brush over loaves; sprinkle tops with sesame seed. Make several diagonal gashes ½ inch deep in top of each loaf. Heat oven to 450°. Place a large pan of hot water on lower shelf. Place bread on upper shelf. Bake 10 minutes. Reduce heat to moderate, 350°; bake 50 to 60 minutes longer. Makes 3 loaves.

Jean Stephenson

Irish Bread

4 cups flour
4 teaspoons baking powder
¼ teaspoon baking soda
2 tablespoons shortening
1 tablespoon butter
½ tablespoon salt
   Buttermilk
2 eggs

Mix dry ingredients, add shortening and work in like biscuits. Add eggs and buttermilk (enough to moisten). Add raisins, citron, currants as desired. Bake in moderate oven about 1 hour.

"The above recipe was given to me by my mother-in-law, Cathrine Hegarty, when I was married 28 years ago. She is from Ireland and is 85 years young."

Helen C. Hegarty

Lemon Bread

3 tablespoons margarine
½ teaspoon salt
1 cup sugar
2 eggs (unbeaten)
1½ cups sifted flour
1 teaspoon baking powder
½ cup milk
   Grated rind of 1 lemon

Cream margarine, add salt and sugar gradually and one egg at a time, beating well. Add lemon rind, milk, flour and baking powder. Pour into greased loaf pan. Bake at 350° for 55 minutes. While loaf is still hot, spoon over bread the juice of one lemon and ½ cup sugar that has been brought to a boil enough to dissolve sugar. "This is delicious! And the secret is in performing the last operation while everything is hot!"

Mrs. Karyl Gadecki

Good Egg Bread

1½ cups scalded milk
½ cup butter
2 teaspoons salt
½ cup sugar
2 packages (or cakes) yeast
½ cup lukewarm water
2 beaten eggs
   About 9 cups sifted
   white flour

Pour scalded milk over butter, salt and sugar. Cool. Dissolve yeast in lukewarm water and let stand till it bubbles, about 5 minutes. Add yeast and beaten eggs to cooled milk. Gradually add flour, beating thoroughly. Do not use any more flour than necessary to make easily handled dough. Turn out on floured board and knead till smooth and elastic. Place in greased bowl and let rise till doubled (about 1½ hours.) Punch down and turn onto lightly floured board. Shape into 3 loaves and place in greased 8 inch loaf pans. Cover and let rise till dough is as high as pan. Bake at 425° for 10 minutes, then 350° for 40 minutes more. Makes 3 loaves.

Mrs. George Nordmann

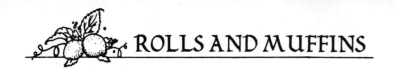

"Dieter's Breakfast Biscuits"

"If you're on a diet and you crave something sweet in the morning, take one slice of bread, spread with cottage cheese, sprinkle with cinnamon, and one packet of sugar substitute and bake in oven at 350° for three minutes or until the cinnamon is brown. It is very tasty and satisfies your craving for sweets".

Sheila Gracin Singer

Butter Pecan Rolls

½ cup shortening
¼ cup and 2 tablespoons sugar
½ cup cold water
1 cake yeast
½ cup boiling water
1 egg
½ teaspoon salt
3 cups unsifted flour

Filling

2 tablespoons melted butter
½ cup sugar
2 teaspoons cinnamon

Topping

½ cup brown sugar
¼ cup butter
1 tablespoon light corn syrup
⅓ cup pecans

Dissolve yeast in cold water. Cream the sugar and shortening. Add boiling water and cool to lukewarm. Add yeast, flour, salt and beaten egg. Mix well. Brush top lightly with soft shortening. Cover and let rise in warm place until double (1½–2 hours). Punch down. Turn out on lightly floured surface and divide dough in half. Roll each piece into a 12"x8" rectangle. Make the filling by brushing each rectangle with the melted butter. Combine sugar and cinnamon. Sprinkle half over each rectangle. Roll each rectangle as for a jellyroll, beginning with long side. Seal edge. Cut each roll in eight 1½" slices.

In each of two 9½" x 5" x 3" metal loaf pans, mix the topping by adding brown sugar, butter and corn syrup. Heat slowly, stirring frequently until blended. Remove from heat. Sprinkle pecans in each pan. Place eight rolls cut-side down in each pan. Cover and let rise in warm place until double (35–45 minutes). Bake in moderate oven (375°) for 25 minutes or until done. Cool two or three minutes; invert on rack and remove pans. Makes 16 rolls.

"This recipe won a Silver Spoon Award in a newspaper recipe contest."

Carol Anderson

Potato Refrigerator Rolls

1½ cups warm water
1 package yeast
⅔ cup sugar
1½ teaspoons salt
2 eggs
⅔ cup oil
1 cup mashed potatoes
7 to 8 cups flour

In large bowl dissolve yeast in water. Stir in sugar, salt, ⅔ cup oil, eggs and potatoes. Mix in flour and knead on lightly floured board until smooth and elastic. Place in greased bowl and cover with damp cloth. Place in refrigerator. Punch down occasionally as it rises. Shape dough into two inch rolls and place each in well-greased muffin cup. Cover and let rise until double in size. Bake in 400° oven 12 to 15 minutes.

Donna Moul

Spoon Biscuits

1 cup self-rising flour
½ cup sweet milk
2 tablespoons mayonnaise

Combine the flour and milk. Stir well. Add the mayonnaise and stir well. Butter small muffin tins. Spoon the dough into tins about ½ to ⅔ full. Bake at 400° for 20 minutes. Makes 9 two-inch biscuits.

Mrs. Coy D. Wilcoxson

Hot Cross Buns

1 package dry yeast
2 tablespoons warm water
Soften yeast in water.
Combine the following:
1 cup milk, scalded
¼ cup sugar
1½ teaspoons salt
½ teaspoon cinnamon
¾ cup currants

Cool to lukewarm. Add yeast mixture and two well-beaten eggs. Add two cups of sifted flour and mix. Add 1/2 cup melted butter and beat well. Add two more cups of flour gradually. Mix but do not knead. Place in greased bowl and grease top of dough. Cover and chill until firm enough to handle. Divide dough into 18-20 portions and shape them into buns. Place on greased cookie sheet. Cover and set in a warm place until doubled in bulk. Bake at 400° 10-15 minutes. Form a cross on each bun with a powdered sugar frosting.

Raised Doughnuts

1 cup shortening	2 teaspoons salt
1 cup boiling water	Dash nutmeg
1 cup cold water	8 cups flour
2 eggs	2 yeast cakes
1 cup sugar	(or package)

Dissolve 2 yeast cakes in ½ cup warm water. In mixing bowl put in shortening, boiling water and cold water. Add beaten eggs, sugar, salt and dash of nutmeg. Then add dissolved yeast and gradually mix in sifted flour into a smooth dough. Place in refrigerator overnight.

Roll out on floured board to about ½ inch thickness. Cut with cutter coated in flour. Let doughnuts raise for 1 hour.

Then place doughnuts in deep shortening and fry on each side until golden brown. Take them out of deep fat and place on paper toweling or brown paper.

May be eaten plain, rolled in granulated or powdered sugar. Makes about 4 dozen.

Virginia Nelson

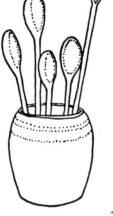

Doughnuts

2 eggs	3 cups sifted flour
1 cup granulated sugar	1 teaspoon vanilla
4 tablespoons melted butter	1 cup sifted flour
	1 cup milk
3 teaspoons baking powder	¾ teaspoon salt

Slightly beat eggs in a mixing bowl, add sugar and mix thoroughly. Melt butter, measure and add to mixture. Beat, add milk, mix. Sift flour, measure, sift dry ingredients together, add to mixture. Add vanilla, mix well, and add last amount of flour. Roll out dough and cut ½ inch thick. Dough is very soft and will stick easily to cutter and board. Keep dusted with flour at all times. Handle gently as dough will fall apart easily. Fry in hot deep fat until golden brown on both sides. Drain on absorbent paper to remove excess fat. Roll in granulated sugar or top with favorite icing.

Suzanna C. Bascochea

Funnel Cakes

2 beaten eggs
1½ cups milk
2 cups flour
1 teaspoon baking powder
½ teaspoon salt
2 cups cooking oil

In mixing bowl, combine eggs and milk. Sift together flour, baking powder and salt. Add to the egg mixture. Beat until smooth. Test mixture to see if it flows easily through funnel. If too thick, add milk; if too thin, add flour. Heat cooking oil to 360°. Covering the bottom of funnel with finger, pour generous ½ cup batter into funnel. Remove finger and release batter into hot oil in a spiral shape. Fry till golden, about 3 minutes. Turn cake carefully. Cook 1 minute more. Drain on paper toweling. Sprinkle with sifted confectioners' sugar. Serve hot with syrup.

Mrs. Lawrence Riggle

Bran Buttermilk Muffins

½ cup sugar	2 cups bran flakes cereal
⅓ cup shortening	with raisins
1 egg	1 cup buttermilk
1 cup flour	½ teaspoon salt
2 teaspoons baking powder	½ teaspoon baking soda

Mix together.

Fill paper baking cups ⅔ full.
Bake at 400° for 18 to 20 minutes.

Vera Kremenak

Applesauce Muffins

½ cup oil	1½ cup flour
1 cup sugar	½ cup applesauce
¾ teaspoon salt	½ teaspoon nutmeg
½ teaspoon soda	½ teaspoon cinnamon
½ teaspoon baking powder	1 teaspoon allspice
	1 egg

Put all into your mixing bowl and mix well. Bake in muffin pans at 400° for 15 to 20 minutes.

Ruth E. Payne

Double Quick Coffee Bread

Melt in ring mold ⅓ cup butter and ½ cup brown sugar. Decorate with nuts and maraschino cherries. Cool before spooning on the dough.

¾ cup warm water	1 package yeast
1 teaspoon salt	2½ cups flour
¼ cup soft shortening or butter	¼ cup sugar
	1 egg

Mix yeast in water, add sugar, salt and half flour. Beat thoroughly then add egg and shortening. Beat in rest of flour until smooth. Drop by spoonfuls over topping. Cover and let rise about 1 hour or until double in bulk. Bake at 375° for 30 to 35 minutes until brown. Immediately turn out of pan to avoid sticking. Serve warm.

Pat Philley

Notes

1 tablespoon = 3 teaspoons
1 cup = 16 tablespoons
1 pint = 2 cups
2 pints = 1 quart or 4 cups
4 quarts = 1 gallon
8 quarts = 1 peck
4 pecks = 1 bushel
16 ounces = 1 pound

Keep baking powder dry or it will lose its leavening power.

Nut Stollen

½ cake yeast
¼ cup lukewarm water
1 teaspoon sugar

Mix:

2 cups flour
¾ cup shortening (butter or margarine)
2 eggs (beaten)

Add yeast mixture.

Roll out like pie dough — 2 sections, roll in a rectangle. Spread with poppy-prune filling or use your own favorite filling. Roll from long side, seal edges. Make 3 slashes crosswise or 1 long cut through center.

Bake at 350° for ½ hour. Makes 2.

Peg Hollaway

Sour Cream Twists

Sift 4 cups flour, 1 teaspoon salt into bowl. Cut in 1 cup shortening with blender as for piecrust. Soften 1 envelope Quick Dry Yeast in ¼ cup warm water according to directions on envelope. Beat 1 egg and 2 egg yolks together until light. Combine with 1 cup thick sour cream, the yeast, 1 teaspoon grated lemon rind and 1 cup currants. Stir into pastry base. Mix thoroughly. Let rise in refrigerator for 2 hours.

Measure out ⅔ cup sugar and cinnamon for rolling. Use all but no more. Sprinkle lightly over board. Place dough on board. Sprinkle over top and roll into 12 inch square. Fold dough from either side to make 3 layers. Roll out again and repeat the folding job, using a little more sugar on the board and dough to prevent sticking. Just remember to sprinkle lightly. Too much sugar and your dough will be too hard to handle. Cut into strips 1 inch by 4 inches. Shape into twists. Lay on ungreased baking sheets. Sprinkle remaining sugar on. No additional rising needed. Bake at 375° for 18 minutes. Makes 3 dozen twists.

Mrs. R. B. Kirkby

Elephant Ears

(a delicious snack from my mother)

3 egg yolks	1 teaspoon salt
1 whole egg	2 cups flour
6 tablespoons cold water	Confectioners' sugar

Beat eggs until very fluffy (about 8 minutes). Beat in water and salt. Stir in flour working with hands if necessary. Roll dough out on well-floured cloth. Knead slightly until not sticky, but still soft. Divide dough into 12 equal portions. Roll each portion out on floured cloth to approximately 8 inch circles. (very thin) Heat liquid cooking oil to 375° in heavy skillet. (About 1 inch deep in skillet) Gently place one circle of dough at a time in hot oil, frying only about 10-15 seconds per side. When turning, and to remove, use tongs and be very careful as they break easily. They should not be brown, but a golden yellow when removed. Place confectioners' sugar in small strainer and gently sprinkle on both sides of elephant ears. They may be drained first on paper towels if desired. Happy eating!

Ruth H. Underhill   41

Sponge Cake

7 eggs separated
1¼ cups sugar
½ teaspoon vanilla
1 cup sifted flour

½ teaspoon almond extract
¼ teaspoon salt
1 teaspoon cream of tartar

Beat egg yolks until thick. Add ¼ cup sugar gradually and beat well. Add vanilla and almond extract and mix.

Add salt and cream of tartar to egg whites and beat until stiff. Add 1 cup sugar, very little at a time, beating often after each addition. Fold egg yolk mixture into egg whites. Add flour gradually and gently fold after each addition. Pour batter into ungreased tube pan. Cut batter with spatula in pan to prevent holes in cake. Bake at 325° for 70 minutes. Invert pan to cool before removing cake.

Merry Biever

Happiness Cake

1 cup of good thoughts
1 cup of kind deeds
1 cup of consideration for others
2 cups of sacrifice
2 cups of well-beaten faults
3 cups of forgiveness.

Mix thoroughly. Add tears of joy, sorrow and sympathy. Flavour with love and kindly service. Fold in 4 cups of prayer and faith. Blend well.

Fold into daily life. Bake well with the warmth of human kindness and serve with a smile, anytime. It will satisfy the hunger of starved souls.

Author Unknown

Caramel Frosting

2 cups dark brown sugar
1 stick butter
½ cup milk

Boil for 2 minutes. Cool to lukewarm, undisturbed. Add 1 teaspoon vanilla and beat until thick.

Mrs. Harold R. Kelly

Gram's Vanilla Sauce

2 cups boiling water
½ cup sugar
2 tablespoons cornstarch
4 tablespoons butter
½ teaspoon nutmeg
½ teaspoon vanilla

Put the water on to boil. Cream sugar, cornstarch, butter and nutmeg. Stir into the boiling water. Add the vanilla and serve warm as a sauce over apple dumplings or fruitcake. Serves 3 generously.

Patty Doorn

Almond Chiffon Cake

2 cups sifted all-purpose flour
1½ cups sugar
1 tablespoon baking powder
1 teaspoon salt
7 egg yolks
½ cup salad oil
1 teaspoon lemon extract
1 teaspoon almond extract
¾ cup ice water
7 egg whites (1 cup)
½ teaspoon cream of tartar

Sift first four ingredients four times. Set aside. Combine egg yolks, salad oil, extracts and ice water. Add dry ingredients. Beat 30 seconds and set aside. Beat egg whites and cream of tartar until stiff peaks form (about five minutes). Gradually pour egg yolks mixture over beaten egg whites. Pour into ungreased 10″ tube pan. Bake at 325° for 55 minutes, increase temperature to 350° and bake 10 minutes longer. Invert to cool for 1½-2 hours.

Ice with Double Boiler Frosting

2 egg whites
1½ cups sugar
¼ teaspoon cream of tartar
⅓ cup water
1 teaspoon vanilla

Combine egg whites, sugar, cream of tartar and water in top of double boiler. Beat on high for one minute with electric mixer. Place over boiling water and beat on high speed for seven minutes. Remove pan from boiling water. Add vanilla. Beat two minutes longer on high speed. Spread on cake and sprinkle sliced almonds on top.

My State Fair Second Prize Winner in October 1971.

Geneva Bratton

Carrot Cake with Pineapple

3 beaten eggs
2 cups sugar
1⅓ cups cooking oil
3 cups flour
1 teaspoon salt
2 teaspoons vanilla
2 teaspoons baking soda
2 teaspoons cinnamon
2 cups grated carrots
1 cup chopped walnuts or pecans
1 cup drained crushed pineapple

Blend eggs, sugar and cooking oil. Sift together flour, salt, soda and cinnamon. Stir in, with the flour mixture, the grated carrots, chopped nuts, pineapple and vanilla. Pour the batter into a 10″ tube pan, ungreased, and bake at 350° for one hour and 15 minutes (75 minutes). Cool cake right-side up 25 minutes, then loosen around sides. Ice with a lemon glaze. Winner of three ribbons.

Mrs. B. G. Troutman

Strawberry Shortcut Cake

Generously grease bottom only of 13 x 9 inch baking pan Sprinkle evenly over bottom of greased pan:

1 cup miniature marshmallows.

Thoroughly combine and set aside the following:

2 cups (2 10 oz. packages) frozen sliced strawberries in syrup, completely thawed.
1 package (3 oz.) strawberry flavored gelatin

Combine in large mixer bowl:

2¼ cups flour — all purpose
1½ cups sugar
½ cup shortening
3 teaspoons baking powder
½ teaspoon salt
1 cup milk
1 teaspoon vanilla
3 eggs

Blend at low speed until moistened; beat 3 minutes at medium speed, scraping sides of bowl occasionally. Pour batter over marshmallows in pan. Spoon strawberry mixture evenly over batter. Bake at 350° for 45 to 50 minutes until golden brown or when a toothpick inserted in center comes out clean.

Mrs. Fred J. Dolaway

Lemon Cheese Cake

18 graham crackers
½ stick butter, melted
1 package lemon gelatine
1 cup boiling water

1-8 ounce package cream cheese
1 cup sugar
1 teaspoon vanilla
1 large can evaporated milk, chilled

Crush graham crackers; combine with butter. Line a 9 x 13 inch pan with half the mixture. Mix gelatine and boiling water. Mix cream cheese, sugar and vanilla. In a large bowl, whip evaporated milk until stiff. Add gelatine; then cheese mixture; blend well. Pour into graham cracker crust; sprinkle reserved crust mixture over top. Chill 12 hours.

Note: May be topped with cherry or strawberry preserves when served. This cheese cake may be frozen.

Marie H. Giddings

Orange Fruit Cake

1⅔ cups sifted flour
1½ teaspoons baking powder
⅓ cup butter or other shortening
1 cup sugar
2 eggs (unbeaten)
½ cup milk
1 teaspoon vanilla extract
  Candied cherries and other candied fruits, amount to suit taste
2 fresh oranges
¾ cup raisins
¾ cup walnut meats

Squeeze juice from oranges, add sugar to fill large glass (8 ounces or more), set aside. Grind orange rinds, raisins and nutmeats together. Sift flour once, measure and add baking powder. Then sift them three times. Cream butter thoroughly gradually adding sugar and cream together until light and fluffy. Add eggs, one at a time, beating well after each. Add flour alternately with milk, a small amount at a time, beating after each addition until smooth. Fold in candied cherries and mixed fruit with flour. Add flavoring. Add ground walnuts, raisins and orange rind. Mix thoroughly. Spoon into large greased tube pan, bake in 350° oven, one hour and fifteen minutes or until done. Let hang, upside down until cool. Remove from pan and pour orange, sugar mixture over cake.

Mrs. W. J. Demerly

Spice a dish with love, and it pleases every palate.

Plautus

Graham Cracker Cake

½ cup butter
1 cup sugar
3 eggs
1 scant cup milk

23 graham crackers
1 teaspoon baking powder
1 cup broken walnuts
½ teaspoon salt

Cream butter and sugar together. Beat egg yolks until they are light and add to butter and sugar mixture. Then add milk. Roll or crumble crackers until fine. Add baking powder, nuts and salt to cracker crumbs. Now add this to first mixture. Last add the well-beaten egg whites. Bake in a moderate oven about ½ hour.

Marjorie L. Barker

Oatmeal Cake

2 cups oatmeal (regular or quick cooking)
2 cups boiling water. Pour over oatmeal, mix, let stand 20 minutes.

Mix the following ingredients in the order given:
  2 cups brown sugar
  4 eggs (beaten)
  1 cup shortening

Sift together:
  2 cups flour
  1 teaspoon soda
  2 teaspoons cinnamon
½ teaspoon salt

Mix together. Add 1 cup chopped dates or raisins, 1 cup chopped nuts. Bake 45 minutes to 1 hour at 350°. Makes a large cake.

Mary Beth Hollaway

Chocolate Cream Cheese Frosting

2 cups confectioners' sugar
1 small package cream cheese
2 tablespoons cream
3 squares chocolate, melted
1 teaspoon vanilla

Beat cream cheese, add cream. Gradually add confectioners' sugar and melted chocolate. Beat well, stir in vanilla.

Donna Kingsley

Chocolate Mayonnaise Cake

1 cup sugar
4 tablespoons cocoa
1 cup cold water
2 teaspoons baking soda
2 cups flour
1 teaspoon vanilla
½ teaspoon salt
1 cup mayonnaise

Combine sugar and cocoa. Add soda to cold water and combine with sugar mixture, along with salt and vanilla. Then add flour and mix. It will be quite heavy. Fold in mayonnaise and bake in a 350° oven for 30 minutes. Cool and frost.

Mrs. George V. Nelson

Coconut Cake

1 cup butter	1 teaspoon vanilla
2 cups sugar	½ teaspoon salt
3 cups flour	½ cup buttermilk
4 eggs	½ cup water
3 scant teaspoons baking powder	

Cream butter and sugar. Add eggs one at a time, beating thoroughly as each egg is added. Add dry ingredients, sifted together alternately with the buttermilk and water which have been mixed together. Add vanilla and beat well. Pour batter into three round or square pans that have been greased and floured and lined with wax paper. Bake in 375° oven for about 20 minutes. Don't overbake.

Filling for Coconut Cake

1 large coconut grated (reserve milk from coconut)
2 cups sugar
2 tablespoons cornstarch
1 cup coconut milk (use sweet milk to make up difference if there is not enough from coconut)

Mix all ingredients in the order given in a large boiler. Place over heat and cool until thick or about the consistency of mayonnaise. Stir while cooking. Cool slightly. Spread between layers and on sides and top of cooled cake. Reserve enough grated coconut to sprinkle on top of cake. The cake batter is excellent even when used with another filling or icing.

Martha Lindsey

Mocha Cake

2 eggs	1 cup cold coffee
1 cup brown sugar	1 cup raisins and nuts
½ cup butter	2 teaspoons baking powder
1 square of unsweetened chocolate	½ teaspoon soda
1 teaspoon each of cinnamon and cloves	1½ cups all purpose flour
	1 teaspoon vanilla

Mix ingredients. Bake at 350° for 30 minutes. Makes 2 layers.

This cake has been our birthday cake for over fifty years and is always enjoyed. A cup of cooked dates may be placed between layers. Ice to suit.

Edna Jaques

Cream Cheese Refrigerator Torte

Crust

2 cups graham crackers (crushed)	½ cup melted butter or margarine
⅓ cup sugar	1 teaspoon cinnamon

Combine all ingredients and pat into a buttered 9″ or 10″ spring form and bake in 425° oven for 5 minutes. Cool.

Mixture for Torte

1-8 ounce cream cheese package	¼ cup pineapple juice
½ cup sugar	1 #2 can crushed pineapple
1 pkg. lemon gelatin	1 large can evaporated milk (chill overnight)
1 cup hot water	2 teaspoons vanilla

Mix hot water with gelatin, add pineapple juice, let cool until it begins to congeal. Mix cream cheese with the sugar. Whip chilled milk in large cold bowl until it is stiff. Add cheese mixture and whipped milk to gelatin and fold in gently, add vanilla and pineapple. Pour mixture into graham cracker crust and chill for 8 hours in refrigerator. When serving top with prepared cherry or pineapple pie filling. Serves 12 to 14.

Marie Bruner

Pumpkin Torte

Crust:

    24 crushed graham crackers
    ½ cup margarine or butter
    ½ cup sugar

Mix and pat lightly in a 9 x 13 inch pan.

Beat the following:
    2 eggs
    ¾ cup sugar
    2-8 ounce packages cream cheese (soft)

Put on top of crust.
Bake 20 minutes at 350°. Cool.

Mix and cook:
    1 can pumpkin, size number 1
    3 egg yolks
    ½ cup sugar
    ½ cup milk
    ½ teaspoon salt
    ½ teaspoon cinnamon

Cook until thick, about 3 or 4 minutes. Remove from heat, add 1 envelope gelatin dissolved in ¼ cup cold water. Cool well.

    Beat 3 egg whites until stiff.
    Add ¼ cup sugar

Fold into pumpkin mixture. Pour into baked crust. Let set. Top with whipped cream.

Mary Lavota

Orange Juice Torte

⅛ pound butter
24 graham crackers, rolled

Warm butter in pan, add crumbs. Pat into 9″ square pan, saving ⅓ cup for later.

Filling

1 cup fresh orange juice
1 pound marshmallows

Melt marshmallows in juice (use large kettle as mixture will foam up).

Cool this mixture.

Whip 1 pint heavy cream. Fold the cooled marshmallows into whipped cream. Pour over crumbs. Sprinkle remaining crumbs on top.

Chill at least 2 hours.

Mrs. David Bullard

Cherry Squares

1 cup sugar	1 egg
1 cup flour	1 cup chopped nuts
1 teaspoon cinnamon	1 #2½ can bing cherries
1 teaspoon soda	2 tablespoons melted butter

Drain cherries — save juice.
Mix in order given.
Bake in 9 x 9 inch pan at 325° for 45 minutes.

Topping

Heat cherry juice. Add ⅓ cup sugar, 1 tablespoon cornstarch mixed with cold water. Add little butter. Cool until thickened. Serve squares topped with dollop of whipped topping or cream and sauce poured over.

Mary Turck

Date-Nut Torte

1 cup sifted cake flour	1 cup sugar
¼ teaspoon salt	½ teaspoon vanilla
1 teaspoon baking powder	2 cups cut, pitted dates
3 eggs, separated	2 cups chopped walnuts

Mix and sift flour, salt, and baking powder. Beat egg yolks until thick. Add ¾ cup sugar and beat well. Add vanilla and mix.

Add dry ingredients and mix well. Fold ¼ cup sugar into stiffly beaten egg whites. Fold into egg yolk mixture. Fold in dates and nuts.

Bake in 9-inch square pan at 350° for 50 minutes. Serve with sweetened whipped cream.

Lois Balerud

Mallow Lemon Torte

1 can condensed milk (chilled)	1 cup marshmallow bits
1 pint whipping cream	½ cup lemon juice

Put lemon juice in milk and beat until stiff. Fold into whipped cream and marshmallows.
Put in 9 x 13 inch graham cracker crust.
Chill.

Jean Crowley

Frozen Lemon Torte

¾ cup vanilla wafer crumbs
3 eggs, separated
4 teaspoons grated lemon rind
¼ cup lemon juice
⅛ teaspoon salt
½ cup sugar
1 cup heavy cream, whipped

Line refrigerator tray with ½ of wafer crumbs. Combine egg yolks, lemon rind, lemon juice, salt and sugar in top of double boiler. Cook over boiling water stirring constantly until thick. Cool. Beat egg whites until stiff, fold in lemon mixture. Fold whipped cream into lemon mixture. Spoon into pan, top with remaining crumbs. Freeze. Thaw slightly in refrigerator prior to serving.

Patricia Drake

Ladyfinger Dessert

1 package ladyfingers (split)
7 — 10¢ size Heath bars
   (chilled and broken into small pieces)
1 pint whipping cream (whipped)

Line a 13 x 9 x 2 inch baking dish with ladyfingers. Fold Heath bars into whipped cream. Place over ladyfingers and refrigerate 24 hours in advance.
Cut in serving pieces. Serves 8 to 10.

Gretchen Handrich

Spring Green Torte

Dissolve:

    1 package lime gelatin in
    ½ cup water

Add:

    ¼ cup lemon juice
    ¼ cup sugar

Cool until slightly jelled.
Beat 1 large can evaporated milk (chilled)
Add gelatin and green coloring.
Line springform with 12 whole chocolate wafers.
Put wafer crumbs on bottom and reserve a few for the top.

Alice Moore

Vienna Torte

3 eggs	1½ teaspoon baking powder
1½ cups sugar	¼ teaspoon salt
¾ cup milk	1 teaspoon vanilla
1 tablespoon butter	½ teaspoon lemon extract
1½ cups flour	

Beat eggs until very thick and lemon colored. Gradually add sugar and beat until sugar is completely dissolved. Add flavoring. Bring milk and butter to a boil and add it to the egg mixture. Then fold in the flour which has been sifted with the baking powder and salt. Bake in three 9″ layer cake pans which have been greased and floured. Bake at 350° for 15 to 20 minutes until lightly browned and the cake springs back at touch. Cool and split in half crosswise. Spread filling on the cut side each time.

Filling

2½ cup milk, scalded
½ cup flour
¼ teaspoon salt   } Blend—add hot milk, slowly
½ cup powdered sugar

Cook in double boiler until thick; cool and add 1 teaspoon of vanilla. Cream 1 cup butter, add 1 cup powdered sugar. Blend into the cold milk mixture and divide in half. Add 1 square of melted baking chocolate to one portion.

Spread the filling between the split layers, alternating the white and the chocolate mixture ending with the chocolate. Sprinkle chopped nuts on top of the cake. Refrigerate until ready to serve.

Caroline Rossabo

Pineapple Torte

2 cups flour
3 tablespoons sugar
1 teaspoon baking powder
1 cup butter (or ½ cup butter,
  ½ cup margarine)

Mix like pie crust and then add 4 egg yolks (beaten). Mix all. Line springform on sides and bottom. Cook together one #2½ can of crushed pineapple and 2 tablespoons cornstarch. Pour into lined springform. Bake at 325° for 45 minutes. Then beat 4 egg whites until they hold a peak. Add 1 cup sugar and ¼ cup ground almonds. (Do not blanch.) Spread over pineapple and bake another 15 minutes, or until lightly brown. Serve with whipping cream.

Frieda Brott

Cranberry Torte

3 cups graham cracker crumbs
½ cup butter
2 cups sifted confectioners' sugar
1 egg
1 medium sized apple, ground
1 cup raw cranberries, ground
1-12 ounce can crushed pineapple, drained
1 cup granulated sugar
1 teaspoon vanilla extract
1 pint heavy cream, whipped

Pat the graham cracker crumbs into a 12″ x 7½″ pan. Reserve ½ cup of the crumbs for later. Cream butter, add confectioners' sugar gradually and continue creaming until fluffy. Add egg and mix well. Place over crumbs in pan. Then combine apple, cranberries, pineapple and sugar and spread over butter mixture. Chill well. Makes 12 servings.

R. Hansen

PIES

Frost on the Pumpkin Pie

Crust –

1½ cups graham cracker crumbs
¼ cup margarine, melted
½ cup powdered sugar

Mix contents, then press into a 10″ pie plate and bake at 325 degrees for 10 minutes. Allow to cool.

Set aside, 1 tablespoon unflavored gelatin dissolved in ¼ cup cold water.

Filling –

3 egg yolks
⅓ cup sugar
1 pound can pumpkin
½ cup milk
½ teaspoon salt
1 teaspoon cinnamon
½ teaspoon allspice
¼ teaspoon ginger
¼ teaspoon nutmeg

Mix well and cook until it boils about 2 minutes. Remove from heat and add the gelatin. Stir until mixed well and cool.

Make meringue of the 3 egg whites and ¼ cup powdered sugar. Fold into cooled pumpkin mixture.

Whipped Cream Filling –

1 cup whipping cream, whipped
1¼ cups powdered sugar
½ teaspoon cinnamon
½ teaspoon vanilla

Put half of pumpkin mixture into the baked graham cracker crust. Top with half of the whipped cream mixture, and top off with the remaining pumpkin. Chill 2 hours to set.

Before serving, top with remaining whipped cream.

Mrs. De Jonge

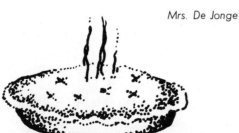

Butterscotch Pie

2 egg yolks
3 tablespoons flour
¼ cup white sugar
¾ cup brown sugar
3 tablespoons water
1½ cups milk
1 teaspoon vanilla
3 tablespoons butter

Cream sugar, flour and egg yolks, add water, milk, vanilla and butter. Stir together and cook until thickened and fill baked pie shell. Use egg whites for meringue.

Iris Crosser

German Sweet Chocolate Pie

1 pkg. German sweet chocolate
¼ cup butter
1⅔ cups (14½ ounce can evaporated milk)
1½ cups sugar
3 tablespoons cornstarch
⅛ teaspoon salt
2 eggs
1 teaspoon vanilla
1 unbaked 10 inch pie shell
1⅓ cups angel flake coconut
½ cup chopped pecans

Melt chocolate with butter over low heat, stir until blended. Remove from heat. Gradually blend in milk. Mix sugar, cornstarch and salt thoroughly, beat in eggs and vanilla. Gradually blend in chocolate mixture, pour into pie shell. Mix coconut and nuts, sprinkle over filling. Bake at 375° 45 to 50 minutes or until top is puffed and browned. (Filling will be soft but will set while cooling). Cool 4 hours or more.

Virgie Edwards

Sour Cream Raisin Pie

Pastry for 2 crust pie
2 egg yolks
1 cup dairy sour cream
1 tablespoon vinegar
2 cups seedless raisins
1 cup dark brown sugar
2 tablespoons flour
1 teaspoon cinnamon
½ teaspoon nutmeg
¼ teaspoon salt

Prepare pastry using recipe for double crust. Beat eggs, stir in sour cream, vinegar and raisins. Mix dry ingredients. Stir into raisin cream mixture. Pour into unbaked pastry crust. Cover with lattice crust strips. Bake 450° for 10 minutes. Lower heat to 350° and bake for 20 to 25 minutes, until filling is set and crust is brown. Serve warm.

Donna Kingsley

Summertime Peach Pie

4 tablespoons of cornstarch
1 cup sugar
3 medium sized peaches

Mix cornstarch and sugar together and sprinkle half of the mixture into the bottom of an un-baked pie shell. Arrange fresh, peeled peach halves with their cut sides up in the pie shell and sprinkle the rest of the cornstarch and sugar mix over them. Then fill the pie shell with half & half cream until it covers the peaches. Bake for about 50 to 60 minutes in a 375°–400° oven. Serve with ice cream.

Sue Harenchar

Coconut Delight

To 4 beaten eggs

Add: 2 cups sugar
2 cups milk, gradually
½ cup plain flour
Pinch of salt
½ tablespoon baking powder

Sift flour, salt and baking powder together before adding:
1 stick melted margarine
1 teaspoon vanilla
1 small can flake coconut

Pour into two pie tins that have been generously greased. Bake at 350° approximately 30 minutes or until set. Makes own crust as it bakes.

Lois Martinec

No-Weep Meringue

½ cup water
¼ cup sugar
1 tablespoon cornstarch
Dash of salt

Combine and cook over low heat until it turns white—*cool*. Beat 3 egg whites very stiff, then fold in cooled mixture. Spread on pie and brown in oven at 350° for 12-15 minutes.

Mrs. Emil Koch

Rhubarb Meringue Pie

1 tablespoon butter
4 cups rhubarb (inch pieces)
1¼ cups sugar
2 tablespoons cornstarch
Pinch of salt
2 eggs
¼ cup cream
1 9-inch baked pie shell
¼ cup sugar

Melt butter in heavy saucepan. Add rhubarb and 1 cup sugar. Cook, stirring constantly until rhubarb is tender, about 10 minutes. Combine remaining ¼ cup sugar, cornstarch, salt, egg yolks and cream. Add to rhubarb and continue to cook, stirring constantly, until thick. Cool and turn into pastry shell. Beat egg whites stiff, add ¼ cup of sugar and place over filling. Bake in 400 degree oven to brown meringue.

Leona A. Howell

Tropical Ice Cream Pie

Pie crust: 1 cup vanilla wafers
2 tablespoons sugar
⅓ cup melted margarine

Mix together and press into a 9″ pie tin and bake at 400° for about 10 minutes.

Pie filling: 1 cup milk
1 package vanilla *instant* pudding mix
1 pint vanilla ice cream, slightly soft

Beat slowly until well blended (1-2 minutes). Pour into crust. Refrigerate while making glaze.

Glaze: 1½ cups (#2 can) crushed pineapple
¼ cup sugar
1 tablespoon cornstarch

Combine all ingredients in small heavy saucepan. Cook over low heat, stirring constantly, until thick. Cool. Spoon over pie. Chill overnight.

Mrs. Tommy Cochran

New Method Custard Pie

4 eggs
3 cups milk
¾ cup sugar
1 teaspoon vanilla
⅛ teaspoon salt

Beat eggs slightly, add sugar, milk, vanilla and salt. Place over low heat, stirring constantly. When steam shows, remove from heat and pour into a 9-inch unbaked pie shell. Sprinkle with nutmeg. Bake at 450° for 10 minutes. then at 350° for 15 minutes or until firm. (This custard pie never gets watery or soaks crust.)

Mrs. Fred Wilson

Puff Pastry

1 stick of margarine
½ cup sour cream
1½ cups of flour

Cream margarine. Add flour like you do to pie crust. Fold in sour cream. Divide in 2 pieces, wrap and store in refrigerator for at least 8 hours. Leave out one hour before using. Roll out ½ inch thick. Cut in 3-by-3-inch squares.

Fill with apple or cherry filling. Fold edges and moisten. Put on ungreased sheet. Brush with a glaze of 3 tablespoons powdered sugar and 1 tablespoon of water mixed. Bake in 350° oven for 15 to 20 minutes.

Eleanor Steffen

Pink Lemonade Pie

1 baked 9″ pie crust
1 envelope unflavored gelatin
¼ cup cold water
1 can (6 ounces) frozen lemonade concentrate
¾ cup sugar
1 cup evaporated milk, chilled
3 drops red food coloring

Soften gelatin in cold water, add lemonade and sugar. Stir constantly over low heat until completely dissolved. Then chill. Beat the chilled milk until stiff and then fold the cooled gelatin mixture and food coloring into it. Pour into pie crust. Chill 3 to 4 hours before serving.

Alice Morgan

Swedish Apple Pie

2 cups sliced apples, cooked
2 tablespoons flour
¾ cup sugar
  Pinch salt
1 egg
1 teaspoon vanilla
1 cup commercial sour cream
  9″ unbaked pie shell

Mash apples slightly, add flour, sugar and salt. Beat egg and vanilla, add to apple mix. Beat sour cream until stiff and fold in apple mixture. Pour into pie shell. Sprinkle over pie a mixture of 1½ tablespoons sugar and 1 teaspoon cinnamon. Bake at 350° for 35-40 minutes.

Mrs. Alvin J. Yoder

Southern Pecan Pie

3 eggs
½ cup sugar
1 cup white syrup
¼ cup butter
1 cup pecans (ground or chopped)
⅛ teaspoon salt
1 teaspoon vanilla

Beat eggs and add sugar, syrup, salt, vanilla and butter. Line a 9″ pie tin with pastry. Pour pecans into crust and add mixture. Bake in 350° oven for 50 or 60 minutes. Pecans will rise to top to form a crust.

Mrs. Austin M. Kay

Fresh Strawberry Pie

1 baked pie shell

Filling: 4 heaping tablespoons cornstarch
1 cup sugar
  Pinch salt
1 cup water

Cook above ingredients until thick. Add several drops of red food coloring. Cool a little and then fold in about a quart of strawberries into glaze. Pour into pie shell. Top with whipped cream.

Joan Glass   53

 # DESSERTS

Lemon Fluff

1 — 15 ounce can evaporated milk
1 — 3 ounce box lemon gelatin
¼ cup lemon juice
¾ cup sugar
2½ cups graham cracker crumbs

Chill milk 3 hours.
Dissolve gelatin in 1½ cups hot water — chill until thick and then beat until fluffy.
Add lemon juice and sugar.
Beat milk until thick — add first mixture.
Sprinkle ½ of crumbs into 13 x 9 x 2 inch pan. Pour in mixture and cover top with other ½ of crumbs. Chill until firm.

Elaine Nelson

Angel Pineapple Icebox Pie

1 cup (small can) crushed pineapple
1 cup sugar
1 cup water
3 heaping tablespoons cornstarch
    Dash of salt
¼ teaspoon cream of tartar
2 teaspoons vanilla (one is for topping)
½ pint whipping cream
½ cup sugar
¼ cup chopped pecans
1 9-inch baked pie shell
2 egg whites.

Combine pineapple, sugar, cornstarch, water and salt. Mix well in a heavy pan or double boiler. Cook over medium heat until thick and clear. Cool.

When completely cool, beat egg whites with cream of tartar until very stiff. Fold into cool mixture, add vanilla and pour into cool crust.

Topping

½ pint whipping cream whipped, add ½ cup sugar and 1 teaspoon vanilla. Cover pie and sprinkle the ¼ cup chopped nuts over whipping cream. Chill in refrigerator several hours.

Very easy and most delicious!

Helen I. Haupt

Peach Delight

Prepare crust:

Beat 2 whole eggs till light and airy.
Add ¾ cup sugar, 2 tablespoons at a time.
Fold in 18 soda crackers crushed.
Add 1 teaspoon vanilla and ¼ cup chopped nuts.
Butter a 9-inch pie tin.
Pour in mixture.
Bake at 350°, 20 to 25 minutes.
Do not overbake. Bake till a light tan.

Drain a 13½ ounce can sliced peaches.
Arrange peaches in crust.

Put this topping over the peaches:

Combine: ½ pint cream whipped
    1 cup miniature marshmallows
        Sugar to taste
    ½ teaspoon almond extract
    ⅓ cup chopped nuts
    ⅛ cup maraschino cherries, cut

Chill at least two hours in refrigerator.

Mrs. Craigen Thom

Baked Devil's Float

½ cup sugar
1½ cups water — boil together 4 minutes and
        pour over
12 quartered marshmallows in casserole
½ cup sugar
2 tablespoons shortening
½ cup milk
1 teaspoon vanilla
1 cup flour
½ teaspoon salt
1 teaspoon baking powder
3 tablespoons cocoa
1 egg
½ cup chopped nuts (optional)

Cream together shortening, sugar, egg and vanilla; add flour sifted with salt, baking powder and cocoa alternately with milk, then nuts if desired. Drop by spoonfuls over marshmallow mix. Cover. Bake at 350° for 45 minutes. Serve warm with a little milk. (If baked uncovered the cake is a little crusty, which is the way we've come to prefer it.)

This is an old family favorite, the origin of which has long been forgotten.

Pollyanna Sedziol

Company Squares

Crush 12 to 16 crisp chocolate wafers with rolling pin to make 1¼ cupfuls of coarse crumbs.

Cream until light and fluffy 3 tablespoons butter or margarine. Add 2 tablespoons powdered sugar and cream.

Gradually work crumbs into creamed mixture. It will still be crumbly.

Spread ½ the buttered crumbs on the bottom of a refrigerator ice tray.

Spread 1 pint of ice cream over the crumbs and sprinkle the rest of the crumbs on top, pressing down gently.

Freeze until firm in the refrigerator.

Cut in squares and lift out with wide spatula.

To dress it up, put 2 tablespoons whipped cream and a maraschino cherry on top of each square.

Kate M. Ownly

Hot Fudge Sauce

½ cup margarine
2½ cups sugar
½ teaspoon salt
3 squares chocolate
1 large can evaporated milk
1 teaspoon vanilla

Melt margarine in top of double boiler.
Drop in chocolate and melt.
Add sugar very gradually (4 tablespoons at a time —stirring).
Add salt.
Add milk very gradually—Water in double boiler must keep boiling.
Last add vanilla.

Cook until desired thickness—about 1 hour, 10 minutes. Can be stored in refrigerator for a long time and reheated. Makes 1 quart.

Mrs. John F. Allen

Recipe Saver

I clip them from the magazine
And from newspapers too,
I gather them from neighbors, friends . . .
And this is nothing new.
I take them down from radio
And file them all away,
From TV cooking schools I find
New dishes day by day.
What fancy menus do I plan
From all the recipes;
O I'll bake this and I'll cook that . . .
The family will I please.
And yet somehow I find myself
Repeating, so it seems,
The same old meals I've done for years . . .
The rest are in my dreams.

Hilda Butler Farr

Sugar Plum Ring

1 package yeast	¼ cup melted butter
¼ cup water	¾ cup sugar
½ cup milk, scalded	1 teaspoon cinnamon
⅓ cup sugar	½ cup whole blanched
⅓ cup shortening	almonds
1 teaspoon salt	⅓ cup dark corn syrup
3¾ cups flour	½ cup whole candied
2 beaten eggs	red cherries

Soften yeast in warm water. Combine scalded milk, the ⅓ cup sugar, shortening, salt, and cool to lukewarm. Stir in 1 cup flour. Beat well. Add yeast and eggs. Add remaining flour or enough to make soft dough. Place in greased bowl turning once to grease surface. Cover and let rise until double. Punch down. Let rest 10 minutes. Divide dough into 4 parts. Cut each part into 10 pieces and shape into balls. Dip balls in ¼ cup melted butter then ¾ cup sugar into which 1 teaspoon cinnamon has been blended. Arrange ⅓ of the balls in well-greased tube pan. Sprinkle with part of ½ cup whole blanched almonds and part of ½ cup whole candied red cherries. Repeat with 2 more layers. Mix ⅓ cup dark corn syrup with butter left from dipping balls; drizzle over top. Cover and let rise till double. Bake 350° for 35 minutes. Cool 15 minutes.

Helen Elaine Boring

Heavenly Rice Pudding

½ cup raw white rice
1 can (8¾ ounces) pineapple tidbits
1 cup miniature marshmallows
10 maraschino cherries, halved (⅓ cup)
1 package (2⅛ ounces) whipped topping mix
½ cup cold milk
½ teaspoon vanilla extract
2 tablespoons maraschino cherry juice

Cook rice as package label directs for softer rice. Refrigerate until well chilled. Drain pineapple, reserving syrup. In large bowl, combine chilled rice, drained pineapple, marshmallows and cherries; stir until well combined. Refrigerate, covered overnight with the pineapple syrup stored separately.

Next day, prepare whipped topping mix with milk and vanilla as package label directs. Stir reserved pineapple syrup and the cherry juice into rice mixture. Fold in whipped topping just until combined. Refrigerate about one hour before serving. Makes eight servings.

Mrs. John Baker

Bread Pudding

Scald 2 cups milk
Pour over 4 cups soft bread crumbs — cool.

Add ½ cup melted butter
2 eggs, slightly beaten
¼ teaspoon salt
½ cup raisins
1 teaspoon cinnamon
½ cup sugar

Pour into greased ½ quart casserole.
Set in a pan of hot water.
Bake at 350° for 1 hour.
Serve hot with hard sauce:

Mix and chill 1 hour:

½ cup butter
1 cup confectioners' sugar
1 teaspoon vanilla

Barbara A. Clark

Flaming Peaches

Sprinkle brown sugar in hollows of peach halves in baking dish. Dot with butter.

Broil slowly until sugar crusts. Put in center of each peach half a lump of sugar that has been soaked for 20 minutes in lemon extract. Light lump and bring to table flaming.

Flo Miller

Schaum Torte

8 egg whites
¼ teaspoon salt
1 teaspoon vanilla
2 cups sugar
1 tablespoon vinegar

Beat egg whites and salt about 10 minutes, until stiff but not dry. Add sugar gradually and vinegar. Beat 10 to 15 minutes longer. Add vanilla. Bake in spring torte pan. Place in preheated oven — 400°. Turn off and leave torte in oven until cool. (2 to 3 hours)

Serve with fresh or frozen berries and whipped cream.

Gladys Biesik

Horns-of-Plenty

2 cups flour
1 tablespoon sugar
1/8 teaspoon salt
3/4 cup butter (part shortening may be used)
Mix all together like pie crust.

1 package fresh yeast dissolved in
5 tablespoons warm water
2 egg yolks, beaten
Mix together.

Then mix first mixture with second mixture lightly with a fork.

Filling:

2 egg whites stiffly beaten
1/2 cup sugar. Add to egg whites
Cinnamon, chopped pecans, raisins

Form dough into ball; cut in four equal parts. Roll 1 part at a time on well-floured board to form a 9" circle. Spread with 1/4 of egg white mixture, sprinkle with cinnamon, nuts and raisins. Cut into 8 pie shaped pieces. Roll as for butterhorns, starting at wide end. Bake on greased cookie sheet at 375° for about 15 minutes. Frost while warm with powdered sugar icing. (Powdered sugar, vanilla and milk).

Note: Although you use yeast, you do not let them rise, it gives them a delicious tenderness.

Mrs. Alton W. Cheney

Cheese-Apple Crisp

6 medium apples (2 pounds)
1/4 cup water
2 teaspoons lemon juice
1 1/2 cups sugar or
    2 cups white corn syrup
1 teaspoon cinnamon
1 cup flour
1/3 teaspoon salt
1/2 cup butter
3/8 pound grated cheese (1 1/2 cups)

Peel, quarter, core, slice apples. Arrange slices in a shallow greased baking dish. Add water and lemon juice. Mix sugar, cinnamon, flour and salt. Work in butter to form a crumbly mixture. Grate cheese. Add to topping mixture and stir lightly. Spread mixture over apples and bake in a moderate oven at 350° F. until apples are tender and crust is crisp (about 30-35 minutes). Serve with lemon sauce or garnish with whipped cream.

Lemon sauce:

1/2 cup sugar
1 tablespoon cornstarch
2 tablespoons lemon juice
2 tablespoons butter
1 cup boiling water
1 tablespoon grated lemon rind
Salt

Mix sugar and cornstarch. Add the boiling water and a pinch of salt. Boil until thick and clear. Continue cooking in double boiler for 20 minutes. Remove from stove. Stir in butter and lemon rind. A pinch of nutmeg may be added if desired.

Mrs. Lester Smith

Grandmother's Baked Custard

4 eggs, slightly beaten
1/2 cup sugar
1/4 teaspoon salt
1 1/2 teaspoon vanilla
3 cups scalded milk

Mix eggs, sugar, salt and vanilla until sugar isn't grainy. Slowly add scalded hot milk. Place in baking dish and set in a pan of hot water. Sprinkle with nutmeg before placing in oven. Bake 35 to 40 minutes in a 325° oven, until a knife inserted in center comes out clean. Serve warm or cold.

Mabel White Epling

Strawberry Marlow

1 12-ounce package frozen strawberries
24 marshmallows
1 teaspoon grated lemon rind
1 cup heavy cream, whipped

Defrost the strawberries and drain well. Place the juice and marshmallows in the top of a double boiler. Heat until the marshmallows are melted. Chill. Add the strawberries and lemon rind. Fold in the whipped cream. Pour into refrigerator trays and freeze.

This is a delightful luncheon or after-dinner dessert.

Nana Beck

COOKIES

Memee's Sweetheart Cookies

"This is an old recipe from France, given to me over 30 years ago by a dear little French lady we called 'The Little Grandmother.'"

    1 cup butter
    2 cups granulated sugar
    4 eggs
    5 cups sifted flour
 ½ teaspoon salt
    3 teaspoons baking powder
      Juice and grated rind of 1½ lemons

Cream together well, butter and sugar until fluffy. Add unbeaten eggs, one at a time, beat well between each. Add lemon juice and rind. Add dry ingredients sifted together, flour, salt and baking powder. Mix well. Chill for an hour or two. Roll out ¼-inch thick, cut with heart-shape cookie cutter. Slightly grease cookie sheets. Sprinkle cookies with granulated sugar. Bake 375° — about 10 minutes. The fresh lemon juice gives a real lemon flavor.

Mrs. William N. Robey

Spice Bars

Bring to a boil:

    1 cup water
    1 cup sugar
    1 cup raisins
 ½ cup butter
   Pinch salt

And let cool while you mix:

    2 cups flour
    1 teaspoon soda
    1 teaspoon cinnamon
 ½ teaspoon nutmeg
 ½ teaspoon clove

Combine the mixtures well and add:

 ½ cup chopped dates
 ½ cup English walnuts, chopped

Spread on greased cookie sheet and bake in a 350° oven 25 minutes. Glaze with a thin powdered sugar icing while warm.

Mrs. Wade A. Bauer

Snow-Covered Gingersnaps

¾ cup shortening
1 cup sugar
4 tablespoons molasses
1 egg
2 cups unsifted all-purpose flour
2 teaspoons soda
1 scant teaspoon salt
1 teaspoon cloves
1 teaspoon cinnamon
1 teaspoon ginger

Cream shortening, add sugar gradually, creaming well after each addition. Add molasses. Mix well, add egg. Beat. Measure flour before sifting, add soda, salt, and spices. Sift together, stir in dough. Roll into balls the size of a walnut. Roll balls in powdered sugar. Place on ungreased cookie sheet. Bake at 350° for 10-12 minutes about 2 inches apart. Sprinkle with powdered sugar before removing from cookie sheet.

Eleanor Cultice

Molasses Cookies

1 cup shortening   1 teaspoon salt
1 cup sugar   ½ cup coffee
1 cup molasses   2 teaspoons baking soda
1 teaspoon ginger   5 cups flour

Cream shortening and sugar, add molasses, sift flour and add ginger, salt and baking soda. Add the dry ingredients to the shortening, sugar and molasses gradually, alternating with the coffee, and ending up with the flour mixture. Bake at 400° temperature. If butter is used for shortening, do not grease cookie sheet.

Mrs. H. V. Sherman

Fudge Squares

2 squares unsweetened   ½ cup sifted flour
  chocolate   ¼ teaspoon salt
½ cup shortening   1 teaspoon vanilla
1 cup granulated sugar   ½ cup chopped walnuts
2 well-beaten eggs

Melt chocolate and shortening. Blend in sugar, eggs, flour and salt. Stir well with spoon. And flavoring. Spread into 8″ x 8″ x 2″ pan. Sprinkle with nuts. Bake in moderate oven (350°) for about 12 minutes.

Pudding powder icing:

4 tablespoons butter
3 tablespoons milk
½ teaspoon vanilla
2 cups powdered sugar
2 tablespoons custard pudding powder

Combine ingredients and mix until smooth. Spread on cooled square. Melt 2 squares chocolate with 1 tablespoon butter. Dot icing with this mixture.

Winnie Donbrook

Chocolate Mint Wafers

Cream thoroughly:

⅔ cup butter
1 cup sugar

Add 1 egg and beat well.

Add the following sifted dry ingredients alternately with milk:

2 cups enriched flour
¾ cup cocoa
½ teaspoon salt
1 teaspoon baking powder
¼ cup milk

Mix thoroughly, chill. Roll ⅛ inch thick on lightly floured surface. Cut with floured 2 to 2½ inch cookie cutter. Bake on greased sheet 350° for 8 minutes.

When cool, put together with:

½ cup confectioners' sugar
2 drops peppermint
3 to 4 tablespoons light cream or milk
Salt

Beat until of spreading consistency.

Gladys Eborall

Chocolate Frosted Brownies

½ cup flour	1 cup sugar
¼ teaspoon baking powder	¼ cup milk
½ teaspoon salt	2 eggs
⅓ cup shortening	1 teaspoon vanilla
⅓ cup cocoa	½ cup chopped nuts

Sift flour, baking powder and salt. Melt shortening and cocoa together, add sugar and milk and let come to a boil. Remove from heat and add flour mixture. Beat eggs and add to other ingredients. Add vanilla and nuts. Bake in square pan for 25 to 30 minutes at 350°.

Frosting

1 package chocolate bits
½ cup sweetened condensed milk
1 teaspoon vanilla

Melt bits. Add condensed milk. (Do not use evaporated milk). Heat bits and milk thoroughly. Beat and add vanilla. Spread over brownies, cut in squares and serve.

Jane Shanck

Thimble Cookie

Mix thoroughly:

½ cup soft butter or shortening
¼ cup brown sugar
1 egg yolk
½ teaspoon vanilla

Stir in:

1 cup sifted flour
¼ teaspoon salt

Roll into balls. Dip in slightly beaten egg white, then in chopped nuts or crushed cornflakes. Place on lightly greased cookie sheet. Make a thimble-size print and fill with your favorite jam. Bake for 10 minutes at 375°.

Mrs. Muriel Hunter

Sugar Cookies

2 cups sugar	2 teaspoons soda
2 cups butter	4 teaspoons cream of tartar
4 eggs, well-beaten	1 teaspoon salt
5 cups flour	1 teaspoon nutmeg

Cream butter and sugar. Add remaining ingredients. Roll not too thin. Sprinkle with sugar. Use your favorite cookie cutter.

Bake at 375° for 10 minutes.

This is an old recipe. They are so delicious and crisp. I have been making them for 24 years for our family. They are so attractive in seasonal shapes plus colored sugars.

Mrs. Alvin J. Yoder

Lemon Bars

Base:

Cut together 2 sticks of margarine, 2 cups flour, ¼ teaspoon salt, ½ cup sugar. Press in 9 x 12-inch pan. Bake 20 minutes in 350° oven.

Filling:

Mix together by hand 4 eggs, 2 cups sugar, 4 tablespoons flour, ½ teaspoon baking powder, 7 tablespoons lemon juice. Pour filling over base. Return to oven and bake 20 minutes more. Sprinkle with powdered sugar.

Nancy McDonald

Coconut Dainties

1 cup butter or margarine
¼ cup sifted powdered sugar
2 teaspoons vanilla
1 tablespoon water
2 cups sifted flour
1 cup chopped pecans

Thoroughly cream butter, sugar and vanilla. Stir in water, add flour and mix well. Stir in nuts. Shape into 1" balls. Bake 1" apart on ungreased cookie sheet in slow oven (300°) about 20 minutes or until firm to touch. Cool thoroughly before removing from sheet. Dip cookies in powdered sugar and roll in tinted fine coconut. Makes about 4 dozen.

Mrs. Gerald C. Hasley

Drop Sugar Cookies

⅔ cup shortening
1⅔ cup sugar
2 teaspoons vanilla
2 eggs
3½ cups sifted flour
½ teaspoon soda
1 teaspoon salt
2 teaspoons baking powder
½ cup heavy sour cream

Cream sugar, shortening, eggs and vanilla until fluffy. Sift together flour, soda, salt and baking powder. Add alternately to creamed mixture – with the sour cream. Drop by teaspoonfuls on ungreased cookie sheet. Bake in 375° oven about 12 minutes.

Frieda J. Hawes

Civil War Applesauce Cookies

"This recipe has been handed down from Civil War times. Grandmother Selden got the recipe from her mother in 1880 and gave it to me on our first visit to the farm in 1925. The original recipe called for 'lard compound' for shortening, and sour cream instead of applesauce."

2¼ cups sugar	6 cups sifted flour
1⅓ cups shortening	1 teaspoon baking soda
3 eggs	2 teaspoons baking powder
2 teaspoons vanilla	2 teaspoons nutmeg
1 cup applesauce	1 teaspoon salt

Cream shortening, sugar, eggs and vanilla. Add applesauce and mix well. Add sifted dry ingredients and blend well. Drop by heaping tablespoons on greased cookie sheet, flatten, sprinkle lightly with sugar and bake 10 to 12 minutes at 375° (do not brown). Makes 44 four-inch cookies.

Mary A. Selden

Cream Cheese Cookies

1 small package cream cheese
¼ pound margarine
Yolk of 1 egg
1 cup flour
2½ tablespoons sugar
½ package chocolate chip bits

Mix ingredients together, adding flour last. Chill dough in refrigerator 2 hours or overnight. Use wax paper to form dough into roll. Chill again. Cut into ¼" slices to form cookies. Bake on ungreased cookie sheet in 350° oven for about 20 minutes or until light brown around edge of cookie.

Aurora Santerre

Mother's Butterscotch Cookies

½ cup butter	2 eggs
2 cups brown sugar	3 cups flour
½ teaspoon baking soda	2 teaspoons baking powder
⅛ teaspoon salt	
½ cup chopped pecans or hickory nuts	
2 teaspoons vanilla	

Cream butter and sugar. Add unbeaten eggs and stir. Add vanilla and sifted dry ingredients and nuts. Mix well. Knead into a roll and let stand in the refrigerator several hours or overnight. Cut in very thin slices and bake about 15 minutes or less in a 375° oven.

Mrs. Stewart Brawn

Chocolate Fudge

4½ cups sugar
    Dash salt
1-14½ ounce can (1⅔ cups)
    evaporated milk (undiluted)
2 tablespoons butter
1 package (12 ounces) semisweet
    chocolate chips
3 packages (¼ pound each) sweet
    cooking chocolate
1 pint jar marshmallow cream
2 tablespoons vanilla
2 cups nutmeats

In a large heavy saucepan stir together sugar, salt, evaporated milk and butter. Stirring constantly, bring to a boil. Boil 7 minutes, stirring occasionally.

Pour boiling hot syrup over both kinds of chocolate and marshmallow cream. Stir vigorously until chocolate melts. Add vanilla. Stir in nutmeats.

Turn into buttered pan (9 x 9 x 1¾). Let stand in cool place to set. Refrigerate if necessary to keep firm, or store in tightly covered metal box.

Mrs. Charles W. Bailey

Most Wonderful Toffee

1 cup butter
1 cup sugar
3 tablespoons water
½ cup chopped almonds
1 package chocolate chips

Cook together butter, sugar and water until mixture turns caramel color or 300 degrees on candy thermometer. Remove from heat and stir in ½ amount of nuts. Pour into a buttered 13 x 9 x 2 baking dish. Sprinkle on ½ package of chocolate chips, and let stand for a few minutes until chips melt. Spread chips and cover with wax paper. Turn dish over and spread remainder of chocolate chips and nuts over top.

Let cool until mixture is hard, then break into pieces.

Helen Rogowski

Christmas Pudding Candy

3 cups sugar
1 cup light cream
1 heaping tablespoon butter
1 teaspoon vanilla
1 pound dates, chopped
1 pound figs, chopped
1 pound raisins
1 pound coconut
2 cups nuts, chopped

Cook sugar, cream, and butter to a soft ball. Beat until creamy then beat in fruit and nuts. If coconut is coarse, grind it. When well mixed, roll as for meat loaf. Wrap in wet cloth, then in wax paper and put away to ripen two weeks, or longer, in refrigerator.

"This has been a family favorite for over forty years."

Virgie Edwards

INDEX

P Q R S T U V W X
4 5 6 7 8 9 0 1